ACROSS THE POND
AN AMERICAN GENTLEMAN
IN VICTORIAN LONDON

R. D. BLUMENFELD

AMBERLEY

First edition published 1930

This edition first published 2015

Amberley Publishing
The Hill, Stroud
Gloucestershire, GL5 4EP
www.amberley-books.com

British Library Cataloguing in Publication Data.
A catalogue record for this book is available from the British Library.

ISBN 978 1 4456 4426 4 (print)
ISBN 978 1 4456 4439 4 (ebook)

Typesetting and Origination by Amberley Publishing.
Printed in the UK.

CONTENTS

A Note from the Editor

Ralph David Blumenfeld was an American-born journalist, writer and newspaper editor, mainly known for his work at the head of the *Daily Express*. Blumenfeld wrote in his diary every night over a number of years; the final result documents one of the most tumultuous periods in British history. The diary provides an excellent first-hand insight, not only into the progresses in Britain, but also into the controversial opinions which surrounded them. This can be expected when looking into the history of rights for women, but Blumenfeld interestingly depicts the varying opinions surrounding the advances in technology, from motorcars to the use of electronic signs. It is clear that there was progress aplenty in this era, but Blumenfeld successfully portrays this alongside the gulf between the classes and also that between the Americans and the British.

From reading this book, the reader learns of what shaped the life of the man who was behind innovations that still continue to this day. Today it would be bizarre to consider the news not being on the front page of a newspaper, whereas in fact if it were not for Blumenfeld this may have never occurred in Britain … or if it did it surely would have occurred a lot later.

It is with great elocution, dignity and even humour that Blumenfeld gives us an invaluable insight into his world and even makes speculations regarding ours by pondering the future of the 'motorcar' and the 'flying machine'.

Victoria Carruthers
2015

INTRODUCTION

The extracts from my Diary, which I present herewith, range across twenty-seven years from the date of Queen Victoria's Golden Jubilee in 1887 to August 4, 1914, the day on which War was declared between Great Britain and Germany.

The time that I have chosen for extracts marks a notable period when vast changes took place in every phase of life. It encompasses the beginning in this country of the telephone age, the typewriter, the motorcar, and wireless. The Victorian era was more closely akin to the century that had gone before than to the one that was to follow. London presented a daily pageant, and the contrasts between rich and poor, the great folk of Society and politics and the 'classes' were distinct and unmistakable.

I have found it necessary here and there to delete passages, since many of my contemporaries of thirty and forty years ago are still flourishing, and some people have prejudices about being quoted in print. Also for the sake of lucidity, particularly to the present generation, I have here and there 'edited' my notes. I may add that I made entries in my book nightly for years, no matter how late or how fatigued I was; until it became a routine of life which was difficult to break. Indeed, it was only due to a long sojourn in a nursing home in 1922 that I gave up my diary.

The quotations in this volume are ended in August, 1914. I thought it best to leave the War period to others or else to postpone it for a later volume.

1887

Tuesday, June 21, 1887.

Wonderful day for Queen Victoria's Golden Jubilee celebration. I spent most of last night wandering through the streets to observe the decorations and preliminary illuminations. The gas-lit streets looked brilliant. Holborn, which with great enterprise has electric street lighting, was particularly attractive. I walked from the Inns of Court Hotel in Holborn at eight o'clock in the morning in order to take up my place in the window at the foot of Haymarket, opposite Her Majesty's Opera House [now Carlton Hotel], but the crowd was so dense that I could get no further than Waterloo Place, facing my window, and there I was stuck in the heat until long beyond noon after the procession had passed. I climbed up the statue of King George, but could not maintain myself and came down. But I got a good view of most of the procession. The Queen's face was hidden from me by a sunshade. The crowd round me seemed to be much interested in a dour-faced, heavily kilted royal gillie, who sat behind. He looked unperturbed and rather grim. A good many onlookers mistook him for the famous John Brown, but he died some years ago.

I thought the German Crown Prince (Emperor Frederick), in his silver helmet and shining cuirass, the most striking figure in the procession. The young Princes, Edward (Duke of Clarence) and George (King George V), were a popular feature in their naval uniforms. It was my first glimpse of some of the Ministers. I had never seen Lord Herschell, the

Lord Chancellor, Lord Randolph Churchill, Lord Knutsford, Mr Matthews, the Home Secretary, nor Lord Spencer, who is generally known as the Red Earl by virtue of his enormous red beard.

In the crowd beside me stood George Giddens, an actor who is appearing at the Criterion Theatre with Mr Charles Wyndham in David Garrick. He knew everyone in the procession, and I was not obliged to refer to my programme sheet. Giddens had been invited to sit in a window of the Opera House, but could not reach it. I recognized one of the lucky ones in a window of the steamship office where I had also taken a place. This fortunate one who had come earlier was Mr James G. Blaine, the American Secretary of State, the famous 'plumed knight,' who would have been President but for the disastrous phrase, 'Rum, Romanism, and Rebellion,' which an ardent supporter of his launched against the Democratic Party, and so lost the Roman Catholic vote to Mr Blaine.

I drove round London tonight in a curricle with Walter Winans inspecting the fireworks. I have never seen so many people, certainly never so many drunken ones.

Wednesday, June 22, 1887.

'Buffalo Bill' Cody is showing his Wild West at Earl's Court. He is living in rooms at 86, Regent Street, over Hope Brothers' shop, and there he finds himself embarrassed by an overwhelming mass of flowers that come hourly from hosts of female admirers. He has had an astonishing success, both 'artistically' and socially, and can now wear evening dress and adjust a white tie with as much skill as he could skin a buffalo calf twenty years ago. He is possessed of a sense of humour too, and laughs at himself as well as at the snobs who are attracted by his titles and his prairie hair.

His mantel-shelf is covered with invitations to 'Colonel the Honourable W. F. Cody'. Little do they know that the highest Army rank he ever held was that of scout-sergeant, and that the 'colonel' was bestowed on him by the Governor of Nebraska when he made Bill a member of his local staff. While the 'honourable' comes from his term as member of the Nebraska State Legislature, which is something like the Essex County Council. They all take the title of 'honourable.' Bill is modest and unassuming. He told me today, 'I've been readin' about Bret Harte and Tom Thumb the dwarf, how they were lionised here for a while, but only while there was excitement about 'em, so I'm taking no chances.'

Am asked to dine and sleep tonight at the house of Mr William Saunders, MP, chairman of the Central News. He lives near Croydon. Rather an erratic old gentleman but most considerate, for he writes to me, 'I warn you that if you are a smoker you will not be able to indulge, for I do not permit smoking either in my house or in my garden; and likewise water is our only beverage.' I am not much of a smoker or drinker, but I think I shall go instead to see Nellie Farren in *Monte Cristo* at the Gaiety.

Ordered two suits of clothes today at Hoare's in High Holborn, rather extravagant in having an extra pair of trousers for each since they cost £1 10s a pair, but considering that they would charge three times that in New York I am justified. Nelson, in Hanover Street, is charging me nine guineas for an evening suit, presumably, I suppose, because he displays a sign indicating that he was coat-maker to his Majesty Louis Napoleon when he was a refugee in London in the forties.

I think it a strange habit for business men of all ranks to knock off at eleven o'clock in the morning and go out to a public house for a drink. I notice this particularly in the City in the neighbourhood of the Bank. Champagne at sixpence a glass appears to be the favourite tipple. Henry Irving has sent me a box for tomorrow night at the Lyceum, where he is appearing with Ellen Terry in *Much Ado About Nothing*.

Had lunch today with Sir William Pearce, the shipbuilder who built the giant Oregon for the Guion Line, and when they could not pay handed her over to the Cunard, under whose flag she went down off the American coast – run into by some unknown sailing ship. Sir William is a believer in big ships. He thinks the 10,000 tons of the *Majestic* and *Teutonic*, now building, will be greatly exceeded, so that we may expect passenger ships of at least 20,000 tons, with a speed of twenty-one knots; electric light throughout, and even lifts to carry passengers between decks. A visionary old gentleman.

Thursday, June 23, 1887.

Archibald Forbes, the war correspondent whose method of transmitting information revolutionised the reporting of important events abroad, took me under his wing today, and asked me to meet Charles Stewart Parnell, the Irish agitator. We lunched at Forbes' house somewhere off Regent's Park. Parnell is best described as a silent, enigmatic, unhappy, emotionless misogynist. He spoke very little during luncheon, ate sparingly and drank nothing. Forbes was telling some vivid stories of his experiences in the Russo-Turkish War, and once or twice Parnell's eyes lighted up, and he showed keen interest.

Forbes was talking about the Ku Klux Klan, and essayed to compare them with the Irish Moonlighters; but Parnell disagreed vehemently; said the Moonlighters were unorganised, sporadic, irresponsible, whereas the Ku Klux were well led, and with a purpose. He questioned me closely about the Irish 'patriots' whom I had worked with in New York newspapers, J. I. C. Clarke, John Boyle

O'Reilly, James Clancy, John Devoy, O'Donovan Rossa and Tynan, the famous Number One of the Phoenix Park murders. Parnell showed little difficulty in disguising his contempt for Tynan's claims as an A.I. assassin. 'Tynan,' Parnell said, 'was never a murderer, nor was he even a willing accomplice, I am sure. In the first place, he was just a poor, unimportant commercial traveller with no political affiliations and, secondly, from all accounts, which you appear to substantiate from your own acquaintance, he hadn't the courage of a slug. No, I think the gang just used him as a carrier of the knives without his knowledge, and now he is successfully making a hero of himself with a certain section of the Irish people ...' Parnell asked me to go and see him.

I had my first experience of Hades today, and if the real thing is to be like that I shall never again do anything wrong. I got into the Underground railway at Baker Street after leaving Archibald Forbes' house. I wanted to go to Moorgate Street in the City. It was very warm – for London, at least. The compartment in which I sat was filled with passengers who were smoking pipes, as is the British habit, and as the smoke and sulphur from the engine fill the tunnel, all the windows have to be closed. The atmosphere was a mixture of sulphur, coal dust and foul fumes from the oil lamp above, so that by the time we reached Moorgate Street I was near dead of asphyxiation and heat. I should think these Underground railways must soon be discontinued, for they are a menace to health. A few minutes earlier can be no consideration since hansom cabs and omnibuses, carried by the swiftest horses I have seen anywhere, do the work most satisfactorily.

Dined at the Savage Club, in Savoy Yard, with Harold Frederic, who persists in predicting a world war, and George du Maurier, the *Punch* artist (father of Sir Gerald and author of *Trilby*), who is also a lecturer. Much amused by the conversation of an old actor named Odell, who appears to be the permanent attraction of this interesting club.

Across the road, in the Gaiety bar, I indulged in the fashionable pastime of discussing world affairs over the marble-topped counter with one of the twenty duchesses who act as barmaids. This particular Juno tells me that her father is a clerk in a City shipping office, that he has been employed there thirty years and that his pay is thirty shillings a week! He has brought up five daughters and one son, and they now all contribute something to the family, though only the son lives at home. The four girls 'live in' where they work. Two are barmaids and two are shop girls, and the combined weekly earnings of the four is £2 6s. The brother is a clerk in a shipping office, and receives 21s a week, out of which he has to buy his top-hats and black coats. These people mystify me. 'Living in,' by the way, appears to be general here. All the men and women employed in the shops live on the premises.

Friday, June 24, 1887.

I wrote to Mr Gladstone on the off chance of obtaining an interview. He is keen on publicity in the American Press on account of their sympathetic attitude towards his Irish policy. Today I have received a postcard written by him at Hawarden, his country home near Chester, asking me to go down there one day next week, Tuesday if possible, and remain overnight. Am looking forward to that. George W. Smalley, the doyen of correspondents here, congratulates me on having 'drawn the old man,' who is usually most elusive.

Everybody here appears to be wildly excited over the experiences of a certain Miss Cass, a simple seamstress, who went for a walk in Regent Street and was arrested and locked up by a policeman on the charge of annoying men.

It appears that Miss Cass is as pure as the driven snow, and the newspapers, particularly the *Pall Mall Gazette*, are highly and morally indignant. Mr Matthews, the Home Secretary [afterwards Viscount Llandaff], is becoming involved, and London's hitherto impeccable police are being severely criticised.

The police, by the way, are really wonderful, in spite of their ridiculous peg-top trousers and heavy frock coats. How they can perform loyal service on £ 1 5s a week goes beyond me.

After lunch I went for a walk with Sir John Puleston, MP, in St James's Park, which is a most fascinating place. In front of us near Birdcage Walk, about twenty yards away, was a young woman most fashionably dressed. She was leading one of those silly clipped black poodles, and was mincing her way along when suddenly and most appropriately in Birdcage Walk her bustle, shaped like a bird-cage, came rattling down from out of her voluminous skirts. She never deigned to turn, but walked on. Innocently – and stupidly – in spite of Sir John's restraining hand, I ran on, picked up the contraption, came upon the owner, and proffered it to her, but she turned on me furiously and said 'Not mine!' and walked on. I shall know better next time.

Came home late after an evening at the Argyll Music Hall in Piccadilly [present site of Troca-dero Restaurant], where I heard a singer poke fun at the German princes who marry into the British Royal Family. Most of the artists appear to make their appeal with songs about 'booze' or how they beat 'the old woman', presumably the wife. The best part of the show was the chairman, who sits below the stage, announces the performers, pounds his gavel for order, and consumes endless and various drinks at the expense of people in the audience who like to let their friends see that they know the chairman.

It was very warm in the theatre. I asked for a long drink of lemonade, which here is called 'lemon squash'. The waiter brought it, lukewarm. 'Will you get me some ice, please?' I asked. 'Get you what, sir?' he asked in turn. 'Ice.' 'Why?' 'To make this stuff drinkable.' And then he burst into laughter. 'We don't keep it,' he said indulgently. I cannot understand how these people exist without ice. I have not seen even a chip of it since I landed. As for ice cream, they barely know what it is except at expensive restaurants. The poor only get ale and winkles.

Saturday, June 25, 1887.

Harry Eversfield; the young actor [he married Eve Boudcault, daughter of old Dion, and formerly the wife of John Clayton, the owner of the Court Theatre], came along to the Inns of Court Hotel today, accompanied by another actor named Chevalier, who is in Toole's Theatre, in King William Street, Strand. They wanted me to go with them to a shrimp tea at the Ship Hotel, Greenwich, a famous resort. You go by the penny boat from the Temple, alongside the new Embankment. But I could not go with them because I had promised to go to tea at the Rev. Mr Haweis' house, Cheyne Walk. Chevalier is an interesting man, and much too talented to stick behind in a stock company at a few pounds a week. He has composed a number of Cockney songs, and sang several of them for me. One of them, 'Mrs 'Enery 'Awkins', ought to be published, and I urged him to do so, but he seems to be a backward, modest sort of creature, and will probably always keep his light under a bushel.

The Rev. Mr. Haweis lives in a fine Queen Anne house boasting a pair of exquisite iron gates. The house is supposed to be haunted by the ghost of Queen Caroline, or some such person. I did not have the courage to inquire, but my cabby called my attention to the left window from the front door. There is a staircase on either side of the door leading to

the first floor. You cannot go up the left one after a certain
hour at night. Something unseen pushes you back. The
curtains and blinds of this big window are never drawn,
and so on. One day I shall look into this. Mr Haweis, who is
a famous pulpit orator and pamphleteer, had a little party of
people, much too intellectual for my conversational powers.
I expected to be drawn into a discussion on Church politics,
but all I could gather was that Lord Lome [afterwards Duke
of Argyll and husband of Princess Louise] should not have
fallen off his horse in the Jubilee procession; that the great
MacDermott has received as much as £10,000 for singing the
song, 'We don't want to fight, but by Jingo, if we do, we've
got the ships, we've got the men, we've got the money, too',
and that a well-dressed young woman was seen last week
smoking a cigarette. Anyhow, I was considerably elated at
my good fortune in being in this atmosphere redolent of
literary history; for next door or two George Eliot used to
live, and Rossetti and Swinburne lived in Cheyne Walk,
too, while round the corner, a hundred yards or so off, the
master of them all, old Carlyle, only recently stamped and
raved at the world's stupidity.

And so, as another diarist used to say, to bed, or rather
to Bloomsbury, where on Monday I propose to move into
lodgings in Montague Street, opposite the British Museum.
I am to have a bedroom, a sitting room, breakfast, 'and use
of bath – if vacant', all in for £2 a week.

Sunday, June 26, 1887.

A remarkable and enjoyable experience today such as
could only be found in this delightful summer country.
John Moore, the head of the Central News, gave a river
party, and had asked most of the members of his staff,
their wives, and some friends. Included in the latter were
Arthur Brisbane [now the highest salaried journalist in the

world, something like £75,000 a year], 'Jack' Wright, the inventor of the 'ticker' which prints news in column form instead of elongated tape, myself and Mr Carey, a cousin of Brisbane's. We met at Paddington at 10 a.m. Never have I seen anything like it. There must have been at least 5,000 people on the platforms waiting for trains. All of them, men and women in white, all wearing 'boaters' [straw hats] and every woman carrying a coloured sunshade. I am told this scene is presented every Saturday and Sunday from eight until noon. We got out at Maidenhead, and there took a large steam launch and went up the river as far as the Duke of Westminster's picturesque estate, called Cliveden [now Viscount Aster's], where we were especially permitted to land and picnic. The river was crowded with rowing boats and punts, and for long distances the banks were lined with houseboats, blooming with flowers. The houseboats appear to be the special summer resort of the well-to-do, who live on them throughout the summer. What struck me particularly was the athletic prowess of so many young women, who were astonishingly adept at rowing and punting, and seemed to be quite capable of handling their boats as well as the men. That I take it is the reason why English girls are so fresh complexioned and free in their movements. It is a fact that you see fewer white-lipped and waxen-cheeked girls than anywhere else, in spite of tight-lacing, which is as prevalent here as in France or the United States. But the women play tennis and go for long walks. They are not restricted by convention as in other countries.

Got back in time to go and hear Mr. Spurgeon preach. He was not a novelty to me, for I have long been familiar with the robustious style of Henry Ward Beecher and De Witt Talmage. There was an enormous congregation of Sunday-clothed people, and Mr. Spurgeon held them as by a string. He spoke of the tendency towards self-indulgence on the part of the people, and pleaded for more effort on the part of the 'haves' for the salvation of the 'have nots'. When we came out of the great tabernacle we stood for five minutes at the corner and watched a pleasant Sunday evening bout at fisticuffs between a couple of well-soused natives, with a good ring of encouraging onlookers and a couple of policemen to see fair play.

Rather surprised this evening to have a call just before turning in from Jeff Colbourne, a famous New York confidence man whom I used to see in the haunts of the wicked in my reporting days. He wants me to vouch before the United States authorities in Great St. Helens that to my knowledge he has led a straight and virtuous life for the past four years. I might be able to make that declaration, since to 'my knowledge' I do not know where he has been. I asked him what he is doing here. 'Selling silver mines in Nebraska,' he said, with just the suspicion of a wink. 'But there's no silver in Nebraska', I said. 'Oh, yes, there is in my Nebraska', and he took from his pocket a beautiful map dotted with red, which are presumably silver mines for sale to the gullible Briton. 'But', I expostulated, 'this is just common swindling. These are "salted" mines. How can you expect me to vouch for you at the Consulate with this going on?' 'Oh, well', he said, 'I'm only doing what hundreds of respectable firms are trying to do. If we can't find silver mines for 'em they'll demand salted ones. They simply must have 'em, and since they will throw away their money, why can't I have some of it?' He went away shaking his head at my stupidity.

Monday, June 27, 1887.

Had the extreme felicity today of meeting a youth who is fast becoming world famous, young Mr Benzon, 'the Jubilee Plunger.' He has just reached his twenty-first year and has come into a fortune said to be £300,000, presumably all in cash, for he is throwing it about recklessly. At this rate it will not last many years. [Actually one year] He is a decent youngster, with no experience and not much brain, and he seems to want to cut a dash – racing, four-in-hand, late suppers, cards, and so on. Consequently he is always surrounded by a gang of harpies who are having a profitable season. I was introduced to the Jubilee Plunger at the Criterion by old 'Pony' Moore, of Moore and Burgess' Minstrels. Benzon had just concluded a bet of £1000 to £100 on Charlie Mitchell, the prizefighter [Moore's son-in-law] against John L. Sullivan in the fight which is to take place in France in the near future.

I was puzzled a good deal today, not being conversant with custom, to see in this morning's *Standard* that 'the Archbishop of Canterbury and Mrs Benson' had been spending a weekend together at Bournemouth. It shocked me to read this barefaced announcement until I was told that the Archbishop's name is also Benson.

Lunched today at Hampstead with Walter Besant, the author, whose books appear to have a greater sale than those of any other British author, with perhaps the exception of Charles Reade and R. D. Blackmore, author of *Lorna Doone*. Mr. Besant astonished me by telling me that the novel *The Golden Butterfly*, which he and the late Mr. Rice wrote in partnership, did not have so great a sale as the later book, *The World Went Very Well Then*, and that the American circulation of the latter was greater than the British. The trouble in this country is that average people do not buy books, but subscribe to the pernicious library system. They seem to be prepared to wait weeks for their turn at a new volume.

There was present at luncheon a tall, extremely well dressed young man, with whom I returned to town in a hansom cab. I noticed that part of his forehead was very much sunburned, but one part, from the hair to the nose above the right eye, was of a different colour. This is

Queen Victoria, 1862.

'the swagger mark' indicating the soldier. It comes from the pillbox, which protects only a small portion of the head and forehead from the sun, a much-coveted distinction. On the way he told me that he is a private in the 2nd Life Guards, and that 'the gentlemen of the Guards' are permitted to go out off duty in mufti if they so desire. A large number of these Guardsmen, however, prefer to go out in uniform, shell jacket, very tight overalls, and pill-box askew on head, ready to be hired for afternoon or evening by nursemaids to 'walk out.' There is a regular, fixed tariff. Household Cavalry for afternoon out in Park, half-a-crown and beer. Brigade of Foot Guards, eighteen-pence and beer. Royal Horse Artillery, two shillings. Other services, a shilling. The fact that there is a big demand is shown by the large number of females at barrack gates early in the afternoon and evening waiting to engage escorts.

Wednesday, June 29, 1887.

I spent from five o'clock until seven this evening watching the spectacle of London society airing itself in Hyde Park. There can be no more wonderful sight anywhere. Certainly there is no place on this earth where there can be seen at one time so many gorgeous equipages, such beautiful horses, and such a display of elegance. Queen Victoria, who is said not to like London, and is therefore seldom seen in the capital, has been out every day of this momentous week. She drove into the park at a quarter-past five – all traffic being waved to one side – in a great C-springed landau with outriders and gentlemen riding alongside. Shortly after she was followed by the Princess of Wales [Alexandra] a most beautiful woman whose great popularity with the people, especially the women, is in no doubt. There were hundreds of carriages, landaus, barouches, victorias, curricles and private hansoms, and such horses! The powdered and bewigged footmen in front and behind the vehicles, the red, blue and yellow plush of breeches, the silk stockings of the flunkeys, the flashing buckles – just like a fairy tale. The great thing to do, if you are a 'blood' and in the swim, is to lean over the iron rails and be recognised by milady as equipage after equipage rolls by in lordly grandeur. There was not a shabby-looking turnout to be seen. It is one of the worst of social misdemeanours to send a carriage and pair into the park indifferently accoutred.

Frederick Wicks, of *The Times*, has invented a machine which casts and sets type. It is not the first of its kind nor the last, but I doubt if type-setting by machinery will ever be as efficient or indispensable as hand setting. Wicks says *The Times* are to adopt his system. They already have a machine called the Kastenbein, which sets type founders' type, but I doubt if it is a great success. I have often had conversations in America with Mergenthaler [inventor of the Linotype] who is optimistic about his casting and setting machine, but, like all inventors, every goose to him represents a swan. I went with Wicks to *The Times* works today and Mr. Wright, the printer, showed us round the subterranean workshops where they actually make the great Walter press. Indeed, *The Times* is a self-contained affair. It is a curiously constituted business, split up into dozens of family shares based on legacies, so that nothing can ever break the control of the property by the Walter family.

Harry Gillig, who manages a traveller's exchange, told me tonight that there have never been so many well-to-do visitors in London, due no doubt to the Jubilee festivities. The fashionable hotels such as Long's [Berkeley Square], Brown's [Dover Street], the Bath [Piccadilly and Arlington Street], and the St. James' [now Berkeley] are all crowded, and you cannot get a suite under £2 a day.

Thursday, June 30, 1887.

There was a large dinner this evening at the Grand Hotel in aid of a charity for widows and orphans, and the presiding officer was the Duke of Cambridge, an amiable, side-whiskered old gentleman with just the nicest touch of a German accent. He is first cousin of Queen Victoria, and missed being King George of England by a few weeks – i.e., if the Duke and Duchess of Kent had not come here post-haste from Hanover the young Princess might not have been born here, and so her cousin, the child of the Duke of Cambridge, would have succeeded his uncle, William IV. So they rewarded his Royal Highness with a good life-long post as Commander-in-Chief of the British Army [they deposed him in 1899], and although he is somewhat of a martinet and exceedingly old-fashioned, he is generally popular in the Army in spite of the fact that the wits insist that he carried an umbrella during the rainy season in the Crimea Campaign.

Before making his somewhat perfunctory speech asking the guests present to subscribe to the charity in question, the Duke appeared to be impatient to reach the speaking stage, and kept turning to the red-coated master of ceremonies all the time making violent gestures. I learned afterwards that he was anxious to push the proceedings towards the smoking and not the speaking stage. Presently the red-coated master leaned over the royal shoulder and then, calling for order, bowed low as H.R.H. rose ponderously and gave the customary toasts, 'Her Gracious Majesty the Queen, The Prince and Princess of Wales and the other members of the Royal Family' and then, in a changed tone, like the rasping call of a sergeant-major, 'Gentlemen, you may smoke!' Then he lit an enormous cigar and looked round and beamed.

The next most important guest was the Right Hon. George Joachim Goschen, MP, Chancellor of the Exchequer [later Viscount Goschen], a tall, bent, scholarly looking man with a poor voice and indifferent oratory. They say he is a genius at figures, and he ought to be, since he was specially picked from a great city house of finance. He, too, has German connections, for the firm of Fruehling and Goeschen, of Hamburg, is world-famous. I was talking to a man beside me, and he told me that practically every big financial firm in the City of London is either of German extraction or has close German blood relations, just as in former days all the financial business was done by the Lombardy merchants, who came from Italy and started business in Lombard Street, where their quaint signs representing birds, fishes, stars, moons, boars, and stags, still swing over the doorways.

I met a most interesting man who lives at Newcastle, a printer in a large way, named Read or Reid. He had with him a Scottish friend, a man named Rawson, who asked me to go with him tomorrow to see him play in a match at the game of golf, at Wimbledon. I have never seen it played, and shall go. Rawson tells me that most everybody in Scotland plays golf – except on Sundays, when they all go to the kirk – and that it is the most absorbing, most exciting, most concentrating, and most healthful pastime ever known; to all of which I lent a respectful but doubting ear, and through my mind there kept running the retort 'Rubbidge!' If it is such a wonderful game why is it that only the Scots play it? From his description it appears that you strike a ball a long way and then walk after it and do it again.

JULY

July, 25, 1887.

Off Queenstown, Ireland. I am writing on board the Guion liner *Wisconsin*, 4,000 tons, Captain Bentley. The purser, Albert Brandt, a jovial comedian, has just been playing the banjo to me in his cabin and singing 'Gathering the Myrtle with Mary – Mary of Sweet Dunloe.' The ship is packed. We have just taken on 450 odd shock-haired, tousled Irish colleens, who are going to America to become cooks, housemaids, nurses, policemen's wives, and senators' spouses. They are packed away forward on shelves, on their own bedding, five or six deep, one shelf atop of the other, and 'when the breeze begins to blow' Heaven help them! For Brandt says that in bad weather the hatches are put on, and sometimes no whiff of fresh air penetrates to the steerage for many days. But they are a hardy lot, inured to a rough life, and will get through all right.

There is only one deck on which to walk. The classes, first, second, and steerage, are divided by a rope stretched across the deck, the first class at the stem. There is no ladies' cabin or boudoir. The ladies may sit, six at a time, in the upper companion-way leading to the saloon. The smoking-room is a ten by twelve deckhouse, holding four green baize-topped tables, with a horsehair upholstered bench running round the four sides. Smelly, swinging oil lamps. Cabins situated on each side of saloon, which is very narrow, with two long bench-like refectory tables. The food is good and wholesome, without frills. All first-class passengers look like tramps, for it is customary to wear your shabbiest clothes at sea. There is no sartorial ceremony. I am told that in some of the ships going to India they dress for dinner.

My neighbours in the next cabin are two iron-grey men, one of them all doubled up with rheumatism, unable to walk, who were brought on board by four detectives, who did not leave until the vessel blew the last signal. The two men are the world-famous Bidwell brothers, the most formidable and ingenious bank swindlers ever known. These two young Americans, one of them, Austin, who is now a cripple for life, was only twenty-seven years of age when, at the head of a clever and daring gang, they came to

Europe in 1873 and began operations, choosing the Bank of England for victim. Austin Bidwell, the master forger, had plotted a crime that involved no less than £100 million. The gang was resourceful and well financed. They had already secured a large sum from the bank by dint of Austin's forgeries, but in the end, after a sensational chase, they were captured, and Austin and his brother were sentenced to prison for life. They were released early yesterday morning after having served fourteen years. Both are prematurely old. I talked with Austin this morning, huddled up in his steamer chair, a pathetic old man of forty-one, who has taken refuge in religion. He told me that for years he lay in a dark, sweating, damp cell at Dartmoor.

'You cannot imagine the hell of prison life', he said. 'Never a smile, never a kind word, never anything but dark, foggy, miserable cold stone walls and food that revolts. When the doctors finally said that I must be removed or die, the warder reported it to the Home Secretary, who sent specially to examine me, and here is the result. I am discharged, but I can never come to England again; nor do I want to.'

Bidwell then handed me a long poem, covering seven or eight pages of foolscap. He wrote it in prison. 'I wrote one like that every week', he said, 'until my hands became crippled. But if I had not written so much I think I'd have gone insane'. The brother has not spoken a word since they came on board.

All the officers of this ship, with the exception of Mr Jones, the third mate, and Mr Brandt, are over sixty-five years of age. The first officer is over seventy, and the chief engineer, Mr Alexander, a tall, bearded Scot, is seventy-two. They are all old-time sailors, and prefer the ship to be going under full sail rather than rely on her engine.

I went aloft with the 'bosun coming down channel and spent an hour with the lookout men in the crow's nest.

There is now a hiatus of three years, during which the writer pursued his calling as a journalist in the employ of the New York. He made many journeys and returned to England for a fortnight in 1889, but this visit was purely on holiday, and produced only the usual holiday diary notes. His experiences as a special correspondent in war and peace during those three years are subjects for discussion elsewhere.

The Diary is resumed in September, 1890, when the diarist, who had been promoted to the editorship of the New York 'Evening Telegram' the 'Herald's' evening edition, was sitting in his office at Broadway and Ann Streets. He had just signed a renewal lease for three years for his apartments 'uptown' at Thirty-third Street and Broadway, when a cablegram from Mr. James Gordon Bennett, the famous 'Commodore,' informed him of change in plans which would completely alter his life.

1890

Saturday, September 13, 1890.

At sea on board *La Champagne*, bound from New York to Havre. ...

I had no sooner signed the lease for my rooms at the Alpine apartment house yesterday, when Jimmy Williams, the negro, brought me a cable from the Commodore thus:

'Hand over to Howland. Sail tomorrow French line prepared not to return for at least a year. Want you to take charge London – Bennett.'

So here I am, bound for France, blindfolded, so to speak. What to do with my rooms I do not know. I shall ask Dunlevy, who has Hyde and Behman's Theatre at Thirty-fifth Street and Broadway, to look after it; or Richard Harding Davis, whose lease will be up next month and may thus care to take over mine. He has suddenly emerged from a cub reporter to the writer of acceptable short stories, and he ought to do quite well. It was just like the Commodore to disrupt me without notice. He dotes on that sort of thing, and I suspect he knew that I was renewing my lease, and so, impishly, interfered by cable. He did the same thing with James Creelman last year. Also when Nordhoff, our Washington correspondent, had completed the purchase of his house in New York, because he was to be promoted to the editorship at headquarters, the Commodore ordered him back to Washington, and then retired him on condition of his going to California to live. I am sorry, too, to leave my *Evening Telegram*, which has been doing very well lately, with a circulation of 70,000, and practically no loss. If I had made a profit the Commodore would have deposed me, but I mustn't make the loss too conspicuous. Albert Fox, our efficient advertising manager, saw to that.

This French ship is totally different in its personnel from that of the British vessels. The sailors do not seem to be so alert. Early this morning when a strong gale was blowing – it still is – the mainsail was ripped clean in two and flapped most dangerously for a long time. The way these sailors went at it make me think that their hearts weren't in their jobs.

Most of the passengers are French, Cuban, Mexican or Brazilian, many of them revolutionaries who have left their country for their country's good. They all make for Paris. Very few Americans or British. One Englishman is on board, dressed in baggy knee breeches, such as one will occasionally see in England in the country. He is quite unconcerned about his incongruous appearance.

The purser has introduced me to a new drink called Martini cocktail, which he mixes in his cabin at noon, before luncheon. It is made of a mixture of gin and French vermouth and a dash of Angostura bitters; most alluring and certainly a better drink than the dreadful wormwood stuff called absinthe, which they sip all day long in the smoking room. I am told that this absinthe habit is responsible for much crime and lunacy throughout France [now forbidden by law].

At luncheon and dinner every saloon passenger is presented with a bottle of red or white wine, according to desire.

We could not drop our pilot off Sandy Hook, after reaching the open sea; weather too bad. The little pilot schooner stood almost on her head while she was waiting for us to send the pilot back to her, but the captain would not let him go, and so to Havre he goes with us. His name is Corcoran. He is a typical Yankee sailor man, hating the French and their ways, distressed beyond words that his supply of chewing tobacco will only last another day, and unhappy to think that he will be unable to communicate with his family for another three weeks.

The pilot schooners remain at sea for a couple of weeks at a time, taking on and putting off pilots. They are small, swift sailers, but hideously uncomfortable and wet – but the men earn as much as 100 dollars a week sometimes.

Paris, Monday, September 22, 1890.

I arrived here last night after a terrible crossing. Had to go to bed at once, and tossed about all night. Am staying in a little hotel called Louis le Grand, just off the Avenue de l'Opera. Just had a most excellent luncheon at Bignon's, which, with Tortoni and the Cafe de Paris, shares the honours of the city. *Escargots* (snails), of course, and *moules mariniere*. I saw a man drinking Munich beer, which is something to be remarked upon, because the French still bar everything German, after their defeat of twenty years ago. There was a riot a few weeks ago at the Opera House, when they attempted to put on an opera of Wagner. Whether it was because of its German origin or because Wagner opera is provocative and not yet understood, I cannot say. Charles Inman Barnard, who is the Commodore's secretary, says there is a restaurant close by in the Avenue de l'Opera, where I can get German beer, but they call it Viennese.

I made my duty call on the Commodore, at 120, Avenue des Champs Elysees, where he lives. He kept me waiting – as I expected he would – for nearly two hours, and then sent Charles Christiansen out to ask me to come tomorrow. Christiansen is the efficient major-domo-secretary-manager, whose father was a boatswain in his master's yacht, *Namouna*. The Commodore took the boy, educated him, and brought him to Paris. He is very efficient, but leads a hectic life.

Paris looks most gay and lively. On the Avenue I saw, for the first time, a bicycle fitted with air blown tyres, the invention of an Irishman named Dunlop. They say that the buoyancy and resilience obtained from the use of this modem invention will make bicycling not only more pleasurable as a pastime, for they are proof against bumping, but that greatly increased speed will be obtained. To me these hugely inflated rims look hideous and cumbersome. Besides, when they receive a cut and the air is deflated, they become quite useless for a long time. Meanwhile the solid-tyred machine, with its immunity from deflation, once more illustrates the story of the hare and the tortoise.

At the Moulin Rouge tonight – a rather rough-and-ready sensational dance and variety hall – I met the great Paulus, the music-hall singer whose rendering of a popular song nearly had the effect of making another Napoleon of the great General Boulanger, whose white horse and white plume were so familiar in Paris a year ago. Boulanger was the popular hero. If he had not preferred to keep tryst with a lady at Clermont Ferrand, where he commanded, rather than come to Paris, where the conspirators were waiting for him to declare a coup d'etat, he might now be Emperor at Versailles. [Instead he had to fly to London and seek death in 1891 at Brussels, on the grave of his loved one.]

Paulus, who is the highest paid music-hall artist in France, told me that his Boulanger song drove the people wild with enthusiasm, but that the general was really made of poor stuff, and could never have emulated Napoleon. 'He was too vain, too sentimental, too theatrical', he said. 'He thought more of his lady love and his beard and his white horse and his great sash than he did of political strategy, and so he had to go under, poor chap. But he came within an ace of it, and we might today again be an empire.'

Sad story.

Tuesday, September 23, 1890.

Called this morning at Champs Elysees to see Mr. Bennett. He sent word I was to come again tomorrow.

Wednesday, September 24, 1890.

Called at Champs Elysees. Same reply, 'Come again tomorrow.'

Thursday, September 25, 1890.

Called at Champs Elysees. Commodore greeted me effusively, and invited me to drive to Poissy for breakfast in his four-in-hand. He drove all the way down. Detaille, the famous war painter, sat beside me; Charles Inman Barnard, Mr. Tiffany, and some three or four strange English and American tourists who were passengers. On the way back the Commodore handed the reins to Fownes, the professional whip, and asked me to sit inside with him and talk business, but he talked mostly about other things all the way back to Paris. He asked me to call on him at 9.30 am tomorrow morning. The only reference to business during the journey was a remark about Joseph Pulitzer, whose world in New York has been making a lot of noise and money. 'Poor, misguided, selfish vulgarian. Can't last', was all he would say. 'He is going to put up a skyscraper of fourteen or fifteen storeys. We'll put up one of two floors, just to show how it should be done.'

Friday, September 25, 1890.

I called at Champs Elysees, and was shown into the Commodore's room by Mme. Leon, the housekeeper. The Commodore was drinking his morning coffee. He had a couple of Pekinese spaniels on his knees, and was apparently in a good temper. 'Please go to London today', he said. 'I've lost £1,000 a week now for over a year on that silly London edition, and I have ordered them to stop it. I want you to conduct the funeral, so to speak. Send all the Americans home and give the British proper compensation for the loss of their positions. They have a funny habit over there of claiming compensation whenever they lose their jobs. But don't worry me about details. There is still time to save the Sunday edition, and if you see fit you may continue it. But don't consult me. It's your responsibility. If you go on with it and lose a lot of money I will hold it against you. If you make a lot of money I'll give you a third of the profits – but you'll not make it. There is a lot of machinery at 110, Strand, where we have been printing the paper, and you will have to get rid of it as best you can. But whatever you do don't worry about it. I hate the very name of London now.'

Then the Commodore picked up his Pekinese dogs, gave me a nod, said, 'Good luck', and left the room. He is a strange, fascinating, enigmatical figure. If he had not been born rich and had to earn his living he would have been the world's greatest journalist. But he has been hopelessly spoiled for many years, and is now just like an Eastern potentate. His word is law.

London, Monday, September 28, 1890.

Had a terrible Channel crossing on Friday, on board the *Petrel*. [A side-wheeled, tiny ship, and very fast.] The hour's crossing from Calais to Dover was so tempestuous that no one could stay on deck; and down below life was not attractive. It shook me up to such an extent that the moment I reached London I went to bed and remained till Saturday noon. Then went to the Strand office of the *New York Herald* and surveyed the wreckage of the late daily. Among the mourners I found the editorial department comprised of Louis Jennings, MP for

Stockport, A. Oakey Hall, former mayor of New York, John Russell Young, recently Minister to Peking, and Joseph Hatton, the author of the amazing book, *By Order of the Czar*. They were not very gloomy, since they had expected the collapse from day to day; so we all adjourned to Simpson's coffee house, close by, and had midday punch.

I have decided to keep the Sunday edition going, and propose to introduce a novelty or two; such as a racing competition and a prize for the reader who gives the best solution in football. Also, I think a novelty will be a whole page for children. There has been a children's corner up to now, and I shall enlarge it to a page.

A good deal of trouble this afternoon with people who say they have been wrongfully dismissed, that one month is inadequate. One man in the advertising department says he is entitled to six months, because he was once addressed as the manager of the department, and that managers are entitled to six months. As he only got £3 a week, I did not mind giving him £78, and he was most profuse in his gratitude.

I have taken rooms at a house in Torrington 35 Square, quite presentable, sunny and well furnished. The place is run by a man who, I take it from his accent, is a Viennese.

OCTOBER

Friday, October 3, 1890.

I only stayed a few days at my lodgings in Torrington Square. It was quite a nice place, but on the third morning the proprietor came and sat with me while I was having my morning coffee, and told me that his profession was that of 'official embalmer' to most of the foreign embassies and legations. Whenever a well-to-do foreigner dies in London my landlord is called in to embalm him. That was too much for me. For some reason my coffee took on the composition of embalming fluid, and on the next night I had a dreadful nightmare, in which I was being scientifically embalmed. So on the following morning I paid up and came to live in Duke Street, St. James'. I have a comfortable sitting-room, a bedroom, a real bathroom – not a portable bath – and valeting, all in, for £2 10s a week.

I do not find many places to dine. There is the Cafe Royal, in Regent Street, a first-class restaurant much frequented by French refugees; Verrey's, a bit more sedate; Scott's, at the top of the Haymarket; the St. James', given over to the jeunesse doree; and Simpson's, in the Strand. You cannot get a meal anywhere after ten o'clock at night, except at old Dolaro's supper club, in Percy Street, off the Tottenham Court Road, where the prices are high and no change is given. Selina Dolaro, his wife, who used to be a comic opera singer, is the chief barkeeper.

You can also get a fair meal at the Continental Hotel, at the foot of Regent Street, but it isn't a very ideal place. If an average Londoner has a visiting friend, he either takes him to his house for lunch or dinner, or to his club. The clubs are usually crowded at seven, the dinner hour, during the season. Just now they are deserted, for 90 per cent of the members are on the moors in the North, shooting grouse and partridges.

It is good to be in London again. I love to sit on the top of an omnibus watching the vista of black silk hats, like dark poppy fields. You can no more separate a Londoner from his top hat and his shiny black brief bag, which every self-respecting Briton carries to and from his office, than you can separate the Ethiopian from his skin.

Had lunch at Groom's, in Fleet Street today, with Mr Cock, QC, a famous lawyer. Groom's is a funny narrow little shop frequented mostly by lawyers from the adjoining Temple. You get an excellent chop for a very small sum. We walked up Chancery Lane and met Mr. George Lewis, [the first baronet], the solicitor who handles all the celebrated social cases: a shrewd quick-witted little man of the world. We talked about the Maybrick husband-poisoning case of last year. Mr Cock thinks she is innocent, and that Mr Justice Stephen, who sentenced her at Liverpool Assizes, should not have been permitted to remain on the bench, since he was himself half insane. Lewis agreed in the latter point, but said he thinks, and so does Sir Charles Russell, who conducted the case for Mrs Maybrick, that she will soon be released from Woking Prison, where she now lies. Her mother, the Baroness de Roques, has succeeded in securing an influential petition for pardon, which Colonel Robert T. Lincoln, the United States Minister here [son of Abraham Lincoln], has presented to the Home Secretary.

Saturday, October 10, 1890.

The Sunday edition, which I retained, is doing fairly well with only a slight loss, and that is due to the heavy charges which the Commodore puts on the paper, with his special fads and 'personal friend' salaries. I have made a contract with Henry Burt, the managing director of Wyman & Sons, printers, in Fetter Lane, to print the paper, so that we shall no longer require our somewhat old-fashioned plant at 110, Strand, and I have sold the two Victory presses, as they stand, to Mr Horatio Bottomley, a city accountant, who is acting as receiver for the Hansard Union, a great amalgamation of printing houses, which came to grief. Bottomley is an energetic young man, who, I learn, has got control of *Galignani's Messenger* the Paris daily, which is on its last legs.

Marcus Mayer, still associated with Mme. Patti, in spite of her retirement, came up today to invite me to Craig-y-Nos Castle, in Wales, where Patti lives a semi-retired life. She has practically completed the building of her private theatre on the estate, and proposes to open it in great state. Signor Nicolini, her husband, was with Mayer, glad, apparently, to come up to town and civilisation for a bit. It is obvious that the British country life is not congenial to this cosmopolitan Italian.

Called this afternoon on Henry M. Stanley, the explorer, who rests between his lecture tours. He has taken a house in Richmond Terrace, and will no doubt make it a perfect museum of African treasures. They say that since his marriage with Dorothy Tennant, the painter, he has become more and more isolated, and sees few of his former friends. I did not, however, find him in the least aloof, but I suppose that is because we are both *Herald* colleagues. He is chafing considerably under the criticisms levelled at him by the families of Major Barttelot and Mr Jamieson, who were officers of the Stanley Expedition rearguard and were both murdered by natives on the Congo. Stanley said to me: 'If they don't stop talking against me I'll tell the truth about the rearguard, and that will not be pleasant hearing for the families of Barttelot and Jamieson.'

Strange to say, on coming away, I ran into Herbert Ward, who was one of Stanley's junior officers. He is a nephew of Roland Ward, the taxidermist in Piccadilly, and he is incidentally a considerable painter and writer. He gave me an inkling of what Stanley is likely to say about Jamieson and Barttelot, and I gather from young Ward's manner that his sympathies are entirely with the dead men. Somehow the great explorer does not seem to have brought home the love and affection of his subordinates, though they all admit his greatness. Ward told me that the world can have no conception of the vastness of Central Africa, which was crossed by the Stanley Expedition. There are millions of black people who know nothing of civilisation; great rivers and mountains unknown, and he tells of a waterfall which is as great, if not greater, than Niagara.

My old friend, Mme Blavatsky, the theosophist, sent me a note from the Avenue Road, near Regent's Park, and asked me to go and have a cup of tea with her. So I went. She says the Theosophist movement, which is run by Colonel Olcott, the American, and Mrs Annie Besant, will in due course swamp all other religions, sects and movements.

The old lady was dressed in a loose wrapper, and she had a great Indian shawl round her shoulders. A large copper lamp glowed on the table, although it was still light, and the floor was littered with papers, photographs, embroidery, and tea things.

NOVEMBER

Monday, November 10, 1890.

This has been a considerable holiday, for it is Lord Mayor's Day, and all London gave itself up to the celebration. There was a procession from the Mansion House down Fleet Street and Charing Cross to Trafalgar Square, and then back along the Embankment, a wonderful circuslike pageant, particularly attractive this year, because one of the Sheriffs in the Lord Mayor's entourage is Augustus Harris, the manager of the Drury Lane Theatre, and he, with his stage manager, Arthur Collins, has made the historic procession more theatrical than it has ever been. 'Gus' Harris, in his green and gold carriage of state, was wildly cheered all along the route, for he is immensely popular. The Lord Mayor, Mr Alderman Savory, is a wholesale chemist, I believe. He looked very fine in the great golden coach drawn by magnificent horses, and drive by an enormously fat coachman in gorgeous livery, all gold and satin and pink silk.

The aftermath of the show was a fine harvest of drunkenness. The Strand at eight o'clock tonight was agog with a milling stew of so-called merrymakers, which means that there was general license and intoxication. The 'donah' girls from the shops and factories, all dressed up in great hats, bobbing with so-called ostrich feathers, find great amusement in assailing innocent passersby with jets of water from little leaden squirts. It is wisest to appear to like it.

I spent part of the evening at a theatre, the Grand, at Islington, to hear a famous comedian called Arthur Roberts in *The Man With the Magic Eye*. He is really very funny and appears to have a clientele that follows him round London, from one theatre to the other. His great claim on popularity is no doubt his faculty of spontaneous allusion to topical subjects. The Cass case, which is still uppermost in the public mind, gave him no end of subject for witticism.

D'Oyly Carte, the owner of the Savoy Theatre, which Gilbert and Sullivan have made famous, and incidentally manager of the Savoy Hotel, on the Embankment, wants me to go and live there instead of staying in Duke Street, St. James'. I can have similar accommodation, bedroom, bath, sitting room, and valeting for 10*s* a week. He says he is finding difficulty in inducing people to patronise the hotel. The restaurant is certainly not popular, but that is due, perhaps, to the failure of Londoners to adopt the Continental habit of dining at hotels and restaurants. At present the Savoy is given over to people from abroad, and they are not many. Carte says that if he had his way he would cut a way through, so that the Savoy could be entered from the Strand very much like Jabez Balfour's Hotel Cecil, which stands up at the end of the little road called Cecil Street. That, I hear, is to be pulled down and turned over to the hotel.

I had a long and rather heated discussion this afternoon with Sir Julian Goldsmid, who lives in a beautiful house in Piccadilly [now the Splendide Hotel] on the subject of a tunnel under the Channel. Sir Julian is a director of the Brighton Railway. He thinks a tunnel would be ruinous to Great Britain. We could be invaded at any moment. 'If Napoleon had been fortunate to have a tunnel at his disposal he would not have died at St Helena.'

'No', answered Mr Montagu Williams, the famous Q. C., who was one of the party. 'No. He would have died in the tunnel.'

Friday, November 14, 1890.

This has been an exciting week of alarms. The Baring failure has produced sensation after sensation and, but for the prompt action of the Bank of England, there would certainly have been a financial panic of the first order. When the news of the collapse trickled out the newspapers found much difficulty in learning the true position, and this seemingly short-sighted policy had the effect of spreading greater alarm and suspicion than the facts warranted. It was hoped that the Bank of England might intervene and help to save the situation, but the Bank was silent. I suggested to Mr. Walter, at *The Times* office, that they should send their financial editor to see the Governor of the Bank and get a statement, but was told that if the Bank had anything to say they would undoubtedly issue an official pronouncement. So I went myself.

Unfortunately I was what was called 'improperly dressed'. I have not conformed to the rule that in order to have the *entree* in the City one must wear a silk hat and a frock coat. I have been disporting myself in a bowler hat and tweeds, while I still further transgress by wearing light flannel shirts instead of white linen. It is something of a fad to be wearing these loose garments, but I am pleasing myself, and not Dame Fashion. I frequently notice that my loose-fronted shirt is the object of comment among people, who think that one is uncivilised unless the manly bosom is adorned with a stiff white shirt. So I presented myself at the Bank and, handing in my card, asked to see the Governor, Mr Lidderdale. A functionary in a frock coat, who took my card, scrutinised me suspiciously, boggled at my tweed suit and brown shoes and my outrageous shirt, and then turned on his heel to fetch a colleague, also in a frock coat. He, too, looked puzzled, but I insisted, and finally they took in my card. In two minutes out burst the Governor himself.

'You are the very man we want to see. We have been discussing the form of statement which can be sent broadcast. Will you help us?' I was taken by him to the Governor's room, and there we concocted a statement, which reassured the world, to the effect that the Bank of England had come to the rescue.

I took the statement to Baron Herbert de Reuter at Reuters', in Old Jewry, gave a copy to Mr McLean, of the American Associated Press, another to John Moore, at the Central News, a fourth to Mr Robbins, at the Press Association (who had already got it from Reuters' when I arrived), and a fifth I handed to Mr Moberly Bell, at *Times* office, and lost nothing in telling him how *The Times* could have had the 'exclusive' instead of leaving it to the *New York Herald* to get all the credit.

Incidentally Mr Lidderdale was considerably perplexed when he first talked things over. I noticed that he frequently honoured me with side-glances and every now and then looked at my card, presumably to reassure himself as to my status as London correspondent of one of the world's greatest newspapers. Finally, when we had concluded the important document, which was to prevent a financial panic, he looked up and asked, 'Tell me, how old are you?' I said: 'Twenty-five.' 'And you are the head of the *New York Herald's* London staff?' I yielded assent to the impeachment. 'Dear me,' mused the Governor of the great bank, ' You are very young to have so much responsibility.'

Tonight when I saw Mr Walter at *The Times* he congratulated me on having secured the Bank statement, and incidentally he expressed surprise at my youth. I reminded him of Delane, who was editor of *The Times*, aged twenty-five. 'Oh yes,' retorted Mr Walter, 'I know that, but there was only one Delane!'

1891

Saturday, February, 1891.

It is becoming increasingly difficult to find variety in restaurants at night. There are only three or four to choose from. So a few of us – Thomas Fielders, Captain Montagu Armstrong, Romeo Johnson, of the US Consulate, Henry Lee, lessee of the Avenue Theatre, and myself – have taken 34, Grosvenor Road, in Westminster, next to the Millbank Prison, the place from which they used to ship the miscreants on board the *Thames* to Botany Bay. It is a row of new houses, and you have to pass through a road of slum houses in front of Smith Square and Grosvenor Road. The house, which is beautifully fitted out, belongs to a solicitor named Wilkins, and he has let it to us furnished at seven guineas a week. We have engaged a housekeeper and staff. Turner, my servant, is to be the butler, and we take possession to-morrow, so that we shall have a family group with a dinner party every night. Henry Lee assumes the responsibility for the house, and we pay him six guineas each per week – extra for wines and cigars. Lee has just produced *Monte Cristo* at the Avenue Theatre, with Charles Warner and Emily Milward in the leading roles.

Loie Fuller, who used to play in Charlie Hoyt's comedy companies in America, came to see me this afternoon. She is very hard up, but plucky. George Edwardes has given her a small dancing part at the Gaiety, really out of the kindness of his heart, and she gets about £3 a week for that. She and her mother are living in a small room at the top of the Victoria Hotel, where, again out of kindness of heart, she is permitted to do her own cooking. Loie tells me that she is designing a new dance with the aid of electric lights, which may be a novelty if anyone will take it.

Went this afternoon with Paleologue, the artist, and his wife to buy her a fur coat. We found one at the London Fur Stores in Regent Street, a long, beautiful sealskin coat, for which 'Pal' had to pay £80, which, considering you could buy them three or four years ago for a third of the price, is pretty high. There were some mink coats for £40, also very dear. Sealskin being, of course, all the fashion now, demands these silly, outrageous prices.

The fur man told me that prices would go still higher to £100 and more, but I can't believe that anyone but an idiot would pay £100 for any kind of a coat, even though he be hopelessly in love.

Colonel Howard Vincent, MP, sat beside me in the Underground today from Westminster to Blackfriars, and explained to me his attempt yesterday in the House to focus attention on the importance of liaison between the Home Government and the self-governing colonies, such as Australia, Canada and South Africa. He moved that these colonies should be asked to confer with the Imperial Government on the question of the development of inter-Empire trade. Vincent is not a great orator, though he is an effective and energetic speaker, but he says he made no impression. 'The trouble is', he said, 'that most of our men in Parliament are noodles, who do not know where and what the colonies are. Anyhow, they moved the previous question, and I lost. But they'll have to invite them in some day or lose 'em.'

Sir Arthur Sullivan has asked me to go next Saturday to the first night of a new operetta, *The Gondoliers*, which he and Gilbert have written for the Savoy. He is most prolific, for on the same night he puts on at Covent Garden *The Golden Legend* and at the New Royal English Opera House [now the Palace Theatre] the English grand opera *Ivanhoe*. Sullivan apparently pins his faith to *The Gondoliers*. Eugene Oudin, the tenor, who has married Marion Manola, the soprano, tells me that he has been engaged to play Ivanhoe. Others in the cast will be Ben Davies, Norman Salmond, Esther Palliser, Miss Mackintosh, and John O'Mara. It will be a great experiment, and I imagine it will finally establish English opera on the grand scale similar to the Continent.

APRIL

Wednesday, April 23, 1891.

I spent a dull, late afternoon in the House of Commons listening to Mr. Goschen expounding the Budget. The only life in the proceedings was infused by Sir William Harcourt, a large, overweight, double-chinned gentleman who is said to be a direct descendant of Plantagenet. Looks pontifical but not royal. He charged the Chancellor with having befuddled the country's finances. Mr. Goschen estimates the ensuing expenditure at £88,319,000, which is half a million over the previous year, and the revenue at £90,430,000, showing a surplus of £ 1,986,000. He expects £13,750,000 from the sixpenny income tax.

I was even more interested in the census of figures of the United Kingdom which has been laid before the Commons. The total population of England and Wales on the night of April 5 was 29,001,018, an increase of over 3,000,000 in ten years. There are sixty-two towns with populations of over 50,000. Population of:

London	4,211,086
Liverpool	517, 951
Manchester	505,343
Birmingham	429,171

It is interesting to see that women are coming more and more into active industry and commerce. For instance, in the City the number of women engaged during the day was 50,416, against 44,179 in 1811. As many as 52,413 persons entered the City via Liverpool Street Station on the day of the census.

Before going to the Commons I went for an hour to the Vaudeville Theatre to see Elizabeth Robin's and Marion Lea's production of Ibsen's *Hedda Gabler*. Both above ladies with Charles Sugden, Scott Buist, and Mr Elwood presented a fine performance of a gloomy subject. They are doing these matinees so well that they propose putting it on at night. In the audience with me was Henry Lee, who is lessee of the Avenue Theatre [Playhouse]. He says he proposes next week to put on a parody of *Ibsen* called *Heredity*, with W. H. Vernon and Fanny Brough; also Robert Buchanan's *The Gifted Lady*. I do not think 'twill last long, for Lee is financially unstable, as I know to my cost, and the actors want to be paid.

On my way home I called on Sir Richard Quain, the famous physician, who is now an octogenarian. Queen Victoria made him a baronet this year. He told me that he had a rough time with the authorities, who wanted to charge him £300 for his baronet's patent. 'So after a long wrangle', said Sir Richard, 'which went on by letter for weeks, her Majesty wrote to me that it was most unseemly for me to quarrel with the officials, who were only doing their duty in trying to collect the fees usual on such occasions.

Whereupon I wrote to her Majesty like this, "Madam, I did not ask you to make me a baronet. You did it without even consulting my convenience. I am an old man and need no such gew-gaws. I'm deeply obliged to your Majesty" – you see she and I are close friends, so I can say what I like within reason – "I'm deeply obliged to your Majesty, but if you want me to shine as a baronet you oughtn't to make me pay for what I didn't seek."

'Well', and here Sir Richard chuckled, 'would ye believe it. Her Majesty paid it herself, but not without telling me that I ought to be ashamed of myself; which I wasn't.'

DECEMBER

Paris, Saturday, December 26, 1891.

Commodore had me over from London yesterday. I went by Club Train [the Club train left Charing Cross at 3 pm], and enjoyed talking with the conductor, Mr Snow [now general manager, Sleeping Car Company, Cockspur Street]. Also on the train were Harry Marks, who founded the *Financial News*, and Davison Dalziel, who runs a news agency [later Lord Dalziel of Wooler]. Commodore saw me early this morning at 120, Avenue des Champs Elysees, and explained to me that since Pulitzer of the *World* is putting up a great skyscraper of sixteen or seventeen storeys, he proposes to put up one of two storeys. 'We'll show them,' he said, 'that we need not let offices in order to pay for our building.' He then told me that he had taken a thirty years ground lease of a plot at Broadway and 34th-35th Street: that he had asked Stanford White, the architect [he was shot and killed by Harry Thaw], to come over and find a Renaissance building in Italy to copy from, and I was to go with him.

I expostulated. I pointed out firstly that 34th Street was too far from the centre of things. It was like putting our present printing plant in the Rue du Commerce out to the Etoile or from Fetter Lane in London to the Marble Arch – much too far from the heart of things. Secondly, I do not think the wholesale news dealers will care to go so far up-town to collect their papers, and we will have difficulty with telegraph and telephone lines so far away. Finally, I emphasised the fact that thirty years was no time in the life of a newspaper, and that 1921, when the lease falls in and the property reverts to the owners, is really not so far off.

The Commodore listened patiently enough, for him, and then said, 'Never mind about all that, Blumenfeld. Thirty years from now *The Herald* will be in Harlem (five miles beyond) and I'll be in hell; so what do we care?'

Then he dismissed me and told me to go back to London and see George Lewis and get him to draw up a paper which would make Reick in New York and myself each a one-third shareholder in *The Herald*, I started to thank him, and just as I got to the door he called me back and said, 'And, by the way, reduce your salary by £10 a week for having tried to tell me my business.

1892

Saturday, April 9, 1892.

Usual scenes in town tonight after Oxford and Cambridge Boat Race, in which Oxford won by two and a half lengths, the fastest time on record. Empire, Alhambra, Trocadero, and Tivoli music halls jammed with rollicking semi-riotous mobs of students. The Strand at 9 pm was pandemonium.

Witnessed a curious, somewhat antiquated scene in the smoking-room of the Victoria Hotel at four this afternoon. I was sitting with Frank Marshall White, William Bacon, Edwin Cleary and Edwin Fox when Captain Harry Vane Milbanke, heir to Sir John Milbanke, came in and spoke to Fox. Both Milbanke and Fox were formerly in the Life Guards. It appears that Milbanke was carrying a challenge to a duel to Fox from Mr Hallett Borrowe, and it all arose out of the indiscreet remarks of Colonel Tom Ochiltree, the famous swashbuckler. Ochiltree had told Frank White that a jury of honour in Paris, composed of the Due de Morny, Milbanke and Edwin Fox, had decided not to permit Borrowe to accept a challenge from one Coleman Drayton, on the ground that Drayton was not entitled to the satisfaction which a gentleman could demand. Frank White, who is the London correspondent of the *New York Sun*, had cabled this information, derived from Colonel Ochiltree. It was a big sensation in New York, where the principals belong to Ward MacAllister's 400. Borrowe resented the breach of confidence by Fox in having told Ochiltree in the first place, and so challenged him today. Fox is a great giant of a man, who has had all sorts of adventures all over the world. Milbanke is a *beau sabreur* who has fought many duels. He was to be the heir to the Duke of Cleveland's millions, but he made an unfortunate marriage in Paris, and so lost it. But he is rich. Should have lived in cavalier times. He is a most charming companion, is said to be a deadly shot and a magnificent swordsman. I have asked Cleary to keep in touch with these people, for they are just romantic enough and daring enough and gallant enough to go in for a duel. Will Bacon, who says he will be Fox's second if they fight, does not think they will. He said, with a yawn, 'I've gone through these alarms several times. At present I'm much more interested in the reduction of this week's Bank rate from 2 ½ to 2 per cent., because that will give me some more credit at the bank.'

Turned in at Romano's for a few minutes tonight and saw the Marquis of Aylesbury, who usually wears coster clothes, with his wife, Dolly Tester, the Brighton barmaid, Charlie Mitchell, the pugilist, Abingdon Baird, the Scottish ironmaster who dispenses largesse with a lavish hand, 'Teddy' Bayley, and several convivial spirits dispensing vociferous hospitality to all who entered. Those who refused to drink were playfully tripped up on the sawdust-covered floor.

Brussels, Sunday, April 2, 1892.

Exciting times. The duel between Edwin Fox and Hallett Borrowe actually took place yesterday noon on the sand dunes of Nieuport Bains, near Ostend, and after two shots both were still alive. Harry Vane Milbanke acted as second for Borrowe, and I performed the task for Fox. Duelling pistols .45 calibre, firing on the count of 'Three' at twelve paces.

I had a great hide-and-seek game for nearly forty-eight hours before I finally got firmly into the event. Edwin Cleary had been keeping me posted in London for days on the movements of the principals. I knew that Fox, who is a friend of King Leopold of Belgium, had arranged to have the fight here, and that in the case of serious result the party would be protected by the police.

On Friday afternoon Cleary told me in London that Borrowe and Milbanke had left for Brussels via Ostend in the morning, and that Fox, Bacon and Frank White were going via Harwich that night. So I arranged that Cleary and I should travel to Antwerp with them. On the boat across I disclosed myself to Fox. He was furious, for he wanted to score off the Herald and give the Sun man an exclusive report, because he dislikes the Commodore. I 'squared' him eventually by giving him an order on the Paris office for £200. If he met disaster at Borrowe's hands the £200 was to be paid to a nominee whose name was given to me. One condition I made was that I should witness the fight. But at Antwerp Fox repented and gave me the slip, leaving me, as he thought, securely and innocently behind at the Hotel St Antoine while he and the others went off to Brussels. But I saw them go and followed them at midnight to the Grand Hotel, Brussels. There I thought it better to attach myself to Milbanke and Borrowe.

Early on Saturday morning we all left by train for Ostend, the two parties not on speaking terms. The police along the route knew all about us and saluted respectfully. At Ostend we were met by two barouches and were driven out to Nieuport Bains, a distance of about five miles. We went to the Prevost Hotel, and the principals and seconds changed into frock coats and top hats. The local doctor with a box of instruments under his arm joined us. The local gendarme kept the handful of excited villagers at one end of the street. They all knew why we were there. Then at eleven o'clock the party sat down to a hearty breakfast of steak and onions and champagne – all at the same table. At twelve we sallied out into the broiling noonday sun, the doctor leading, then Cleary, Fox, Milbanke, Borrowe, Frank White, myself, and, rather shakily, Bacon, far behind. The sun and the champagne and the thirty-four hours of excitement had affected him so that on the way to the dunes he resigned as second and became a mere onlooker. I was selected to second for Fox.

The sand dunes, where we pitched, were like deep bowls. The sun poured straight down on the white sand and blinded us a good deal. Bacon went to sleep on the ground. White, Cleary and the doctor got out of reach, as they thought, and sat on the rim of the dune above us. Milbanke and I loaded the beautiful pistols and, rammed down the charges. The order was twelve paces, side sighting to fire on the order 'One, two, three,' and firing between 'two and three.'

Fox's first shot, aimed high, whistled between Cleary and the doctor above, and they quickly disappeared from sight on the other side of the rim. I went up to Fox, and he asked for a cigarette. Borrowe's bullet had torn the nap of his buttoned frock coat, just scraping across. He began to smoke, as cool as a duck. We loaded and fired again. No result. The blinding sun on the sand made it difficult for the men to see clearly. Milbanke said that was enough, since honour was satisfied. I suggested reconciliation, but they both rejected that, and so the two parties broke up. Most of them took the steamer for Dover.

I went with Milbanke to Brussels to the Grand Hotel, and as I had not enough money to pay for the cablegram I was sending, Milbanke lent me a thousand francs, although he objects to newspapers.

DECEMBER

Friday, December 13, 1892.

Funny incident this afternoon in St. James's Square. I got a cablegram from Clancy, the foreign editor in New York, asking me to try and get some information from the Foreign

Office about a report of a proposed naval demonstration in Egypt in order to impress the Khedive. The cablegram added, 'Interview Gladstone, if possible.' I knew, of course, that the P. M. would not be interviewed, so I determined on the next course – namely, to send a good informative message about the British Fleet, its armaments, foot-seconds sort of statistics.

There is a good naval library at the Junior Travellers' Club in St. James's Square [now the Sports Club], and thither I repaired to make up my despatch.

Just as I came out of Charles Street into St. James's Square I spied the Prime Minister walking round by the iron railings opposite, apparently bent on an after-lunch walk. He had a big grey shawl over his shoulders, and appeared to be talking to himself. The usual Scotland Yard 'shadow' was not there, so I concluded the P. M. was only out for a few minutes. But it appeared to me to be providential, and so, since Mr. Gladstone knows me well and is always most friendly to me, I stepped across, and, raising my silk hat, said, 'Good day, Prime Minister. I – '

'Go away,' said the P. M., without looking up, and walked on. I stepped alongside, and said, 'But, Mr Gladstone, you don't appear to know me. I am Blumenfeld, of the *New York Herald*, and I would like – ' The old man stood still and glared like a ferocious lion. 'Go away, I tell you,' he added. 'I don't know you. Don't bother me,' and stumped on.

The old apple woman sitting beside her basket opposite the Duke of Norfolk's house jeered at me. A cabman on his hansom cracked his whip at me; and I sneaked across to the club. I am sure that tomorrow I shall have a postcard from the P. M. asking me to overlook it. [I never got it]

I went to Bond Street Police Court this morning with Arthur Pearson to hear Sir John Bridge, the chief magistrate, pronounce missing word competitions as illegal. This will be a blow not only to Pearson, who invented these competitions,

Hon. William Gladstone, 1913.

but also to the Harmsworth brothers [Northcliffe and Rothermere] and George Newnes, who all base their fortunes on this style of weekly circulation getting. Pearson says at one time the replies came in so thick and fast with shilling postal orders enclosed that it was impossible to keep control. Office boys were found with their pockets stuffed with postal orders. Those that were crossed they shoved down the drains and choked them up. Pearson says that the Harmsworths must be making £50,000 a year clear. Three or four years ago they were poor.

Willie Walrond tells me tonight he understands that Jabez Balfour, the head of the great Liberator Company, has resigned his seat owing to the charges of fraud that are being levelled against him and his colleagues. I met Balfour some months ago. He looked to me like a smug customer, and I shall not be surprised if he runs away before they have the law on him. The ruin that has been brought on thousands of poor people who have lost their savings in Balfour's companies is incalculable.

1893–97

In January, 1893, the Diarist was suddenly ordered to New York by Mr James Gordon Bennett to take charge of the construction of the new Renaissance building and to assume the duties of business manager, with which he was wholly unfamiliar, since he was a journalist untrained to business methods. year in America brought the completion of the building, after which, desiring to live in England, he returned here to form a company to manufacture typesetting machines, which were just then coming into use. But in spite of the absorption due to the claims of a great manufacturing business, his heart was in journalism, and for six years he contributed to many papers and frequently acted as a special correspondent.

Thus, for instance, the opening of the Kiel Canal, in which there was an interview with the All Highest on board the Imperial *yacht in June, 1895; the funeral of President Carnot, for the New York 'American'; Mr Hiram Maxim's flying machine at Bexley; a trip with Beerbohm Tree to Balmoral to do a special performance of 'The Ballad Monger' and 'Red Lamp.'*

It is deemed unnecessary to give many details from the Diary from 1894 to 1899. It was not a transition period, and the Diarist was not so much in touch with the great world as he was during his journalistic days before and after.

Only here and there in the Diary are there entries which indicate the manners, modes and customs, such, for instance, as an entry in June, 1896, when it was fashionable for society to go bicycling and breakfasting in Battersea Park in the mornings. Here is a specimen:

June 16, 1896.

I went across Albert Bridge from Cheyne Court at 9.45 a.m. The Park road was already full of bicyclists, and many were already having coffee and rolls. I rode for a while with General [afterwards Field-Marshal] Sir Evelyn Wood and Sir Francis Jeune, the divorce judge [Lord St Helier], Colonel Brabazon [Major-General Sir John], Mr Claude Lowther, Mr Sidney Greville, Lady Sykes [Jessica], who rides a horse better than she does a bicycle, Mrs Brown Potter, the actress, Lady Essex, Princess Dolgorouki, Mr Lewis Waller, the actor, and so on. Mr Henry Chaplin stood on the sidewalk looking on. He told me he prefers to ride an 18-hand high horse that hasn't got wobbly wheels.

In June 1896, there was also a visit to Tunbridge Wells to inspect a number of horseless carriages (motorcars), which were put on exhibition by the Mayor, Sir David Salomons. The new invention was generally derided. Besides, the law required that a man with a red flag should always precede a mechanically driven vehicle on the road.

In August, 1896, there is an entry of a conversation with Li Hung Chang, the famous statesman, at the Chinese Legation in Portland Place, where he was staying. Here is the entry:

Sir Halliday MacCartney arranged an interview for me with Li Hung Chang. It lasted twenty minutes. The old man was gorgeously dressed in sky blue. He eyed me quizzically for a time and then asked quickly, hardly giving me time to answer: 'How old are you? How much money have you got? How much do you earn? Phew! [Or words to that effect] That's a lot of money! Are you married? How many children? How old is your father? Your mother? Do you live in a house with a garden? How many servants do you keep? Do you smoke?' and so on. He simply would not get down to business, and I could get nothing from him on the Shimoniseki (Japanese) peace treaty. A weird old bird. They say he is worth over £30 million.

June 12, 1897.

I witnessed Queen Victoria's progress in her Diamond Jubilee Procession from Buckingham Palace to St. Paul's, via South London. I saw the return journey pass Chancery Lane and Fleet. Street from a window in a stationer's shop. Colonel Jack Cowans in Rifleman's Uniform [Lieut. General Sir John S. Cowans, war time – Quartermaster – General] led the military, which was composed of a fine selection of British, Indian, and other troops from the Seven Seas; Prime Ministers from a dozen colonies; the German Emperor and all sorts of potentates; but I liked best the popular figure of Field-Marshal Lord Roberts, VC, on his white charger. He got almost as many cheers as the Queen.

Tuesday, June 2, 1896.

For some time past I have been receiving letters and telegrams from Joseph Pulitzer, the blind proprietor of the New York *World*, suggesting that I should join his staff in an executive capacity. I have constantly turned down these invitations, because I am not enamoured of the style of journalism represented by the Pulitzer school. Mr Carvalho, who is Mr Pulitzer's principal aide and an old colleague of mine, states that I can have the choice of Managing Editorship of the Morning *World* or the Evening *World*, or charge of the *Post-Despatch* in St. Louis. Still I remain outside. Finally, since Mr Ballard Smith, the London correspondent, is on the point of retiring, Mr Pulitzer asks me to take up that post. I got a note yesterday from Mr Butes, the efficient English secretary, asking me to lunch today at Moray Lodge, Campden Hill, where 'J. P.' has entrenched himself with his secretariat, which includes Dr. Hosmer, formerly Editor of the *Herald*, and David Graham Phillips [subsequently assassinated in Gramercy Park, New York, by a madman], I went to lunch.

'J. P.,' Dr Hosmer, Phillips, Sam Williams, and myself. 'J. P.' very petulant because Dr Hosmer refused him permission to eat certain dishes. I sat next to him, and he pelted me with questions. Talk ranged from metaphysics to spiritualism, murder trials and police reporting. A man with a most astonishing range of conversation. Tall, cadaverous, reddish beard, and hair growing grey, piercing but dead eyes, long bony hands: a fascinating yet terrifying figure. He is not quite blind, but cannot see to read even with the most powerful glasses.

After lunch 'J. P.' took me for a drive in a Victoria. We drove through Kensington to Chelsea, over Chelsea Bridge to Battersea Park. All the way he was bombarding me with questions about the *Herald*'s interior mechanism, its personalities, its office politics, its revenues, and so on; and throughout I attempted to dodge him. He was obviously bent on getting inside information, and I was bent on not telling him, even though I am no longer a *Herald* man. Eventually, after we had driven round the park five or six times we came back into Chelsea.

'You are not very communicative,' said Mr Pulitzer. 'I expect when you've joined the *World* you will be more so. Now when will you be ready to take over Mr Ballard Smith's duties as London correspondent?'

'Excuse me, Mr Pulitzer,' I retorted. 'I have never said I would join your staff. I do not want to do so.'

'Why not, please?' I could see his colour rising.

'Because I choose not to be on the *World*,' I answered. 'At least not at present.'

'J. P.' did a characteristic thing. He sat up straight in the Victoria, lifted his stick, poked the coachman in the back, and said, 'Stop, please. This gentleman is getting out here.'

So, at the corner of the King's Road I got out and took a hansom: and that's how I didn't join the *World*.

1900–01

October 1, 1900.

Lord Salisbury has no qualms about the election. I saw his great, bulky, stooping form coming down Birdcage Walk, his beard rather unkempt and his great hat obviously in need of a brushing. When he saw me he stopped and waved his old umbrella. 'Did you see what Campbell-Bannerman has said about a Liberal victory in the offing?' he said. 'He isn't usually so foolhardy. We are going to have a great majority. I see that Arthur Balfour and Asquith and Brodrick have all been eulogising Lord Roberts. So they should. He is a great man, but they might have added that he and the soldiers have caused the election; not I.'

I saw Claude Hay, brother of Lord Kinnoull, in Dover Street sitting in a large motorcar with a tonneau body. He informs me he is off to Leicestershire to help a friend in the election, and has adopted this novel vehicle as a method of taking people to the polls. A motor-car maker tells me that he will not be surprised if motorcars are used in future as much as horses. *The Daily Express* has issued a warning on the dangers of motoring, for these machines are not to be handled on a casual acquaintance. The man who is taking a precious load of voters to the poll in support of a candidate ought to be above suspicion as to sobriety and skill in working the mechanism.

The wedding of Miss Constance Gore-Booth, daughter of the late Sir Henry Gore-Booth, to Count Casimir de Markieviecz, of Poland, at Marylebone Church, was picturesque. The bridegroom wore full Russian Court dress, and as he speaks no English, the bride translated the responses into Russian for him. She is a clever but rather erratic girl who prefers to talk Irish politics.

Lady Londonderry, who is still a great beauty, came to town today from Wynyard. She told me that she has heard that Mr W. K. Vanderbilt has just presented his daughter, the Duchess of Marlborough, with a cheque for 500,000 dollars to celebrate the safe return of the duke from the war. The new house in Curzon Street which the duchess is building will soon be finished. Lady L. – everyone speaks of her thus – said, with an assumed appearance of ruefulness, 'I suppose when the palace is finished my position as hostess will be challenged.' I doubt that. Lady L.'s position as leader of society will probably never be taken by anyone.

Beerbohm Tree sends me a note asking if I will not aid in asking ladies to take off their large picture hats in the theatre. 'They won't mind, I am sure,' he adds. 'Women don't mind much nowadays anyhow what they do in public. Look at them smoking cigarettes in restaurants!' I do not find smoking general among women. It is confined to three kinds, the 'smart set,' bachelor girls, and actresses. Mr Burbidge, of Harrods, told me the other day that one of his girls was dismissed from Harrods for smoking.

I looked in at the Empire last night and saw some Boer War pictures on the bioscope. They were very lifelike, and almost free from flicker, which usually makes these moving pictures so objectionable.

Sir John Blundell Maple, of Tottenham Court Road, is not at all pleased at getting in for Dulwich without a contest in the general election. He asserted to me today that he had been spoiling for a fight. He had got his familiar fine four-in-hand all ready to tour the constituency, and I presume one of his reasons for wanting to face his electors was that if they questioned him as to his voting last session he would be ready to 'furnish' explanations.

Lord Camavon is becoming a public nuisance as a motor scorcher. He was summoned again today. Clouds of dust as high as the neighbouring trees, said the police witnesses, rose up as his car whizzed along the road. By careful timing and measurements the superintendent calculated the rate of speed at a mile in two and a half minutes, or twenty-four miles an hour!

Frank Butler, the hon. secretary of the Automobile Club in Piccadilly, is very angry with the police. They haled him before the New Romney magistrates yesterday for scorching in his new Panhard at eighteen miles per hour; but he got off.

At the War Office they say that Lieutenant Claude Lowther, of the Cumberland Yeomanry, has been recommended for the VC for a gallant action in Natal; but I do not think he will get it, for Sir Redvers Buller had a series of rows with Sir Charles Warren, the ex-Commissioner of Police, who commanded under Buller, and who recommended Lowther, and Buller does not agree with Warren's ideas on most subjects. Young Mr Lowther has, I hear, Parliamentary aspirations, and he should have little difficulty in getting one of the Lowther seats in Cumberland.

Sir Evelyn Wood, the Adjutant-General, who grows more deaf every day, showed me a sample of the new bearskin hat of the newly formed Irish Guards. It has a big blue plume. The regiment is to be called the 4th Guards Regiment of the Household Brigade.

When I left the War Office Sir Evelyn came out of the door with me and whispered that Mr Brodrick, the War Secretary [now Earl of Midleton], was not at all agreeable to the visits of myself and one or two other editors to the Adjutant-General's office. In fact, he was arranging to put in a sort of super-press agent to whom all journalists will have to go in future. Sir Evelyn thinks it will be Colonel Edward Ward [late Sir Edward], the man who fed Ladysmith during the siege and whom Lord Roberts eulogised as 'the best supply officer since Moses.' Sir Evelyn says Ward, who is a handsome, suave and tactful man, will probably soon succeed Sir Ralph Knox as permanent secretary. [He succeeded in 1901.]

The Countess of Warwick writes to me from Scotland that she declines any longer to be numbered among the Tory electioneering workers. She tells her friends that she wants no more party politics.

Ladies who persist in riding bicycles in long skirts must expect to get hurt. I saw a handsome Junoesque figure today [Mrs Sands], dressed in laces and flounces, riding on a bicycle in Sloane Street. Her skirt became entangled and she came down with a crash. My tailor tells me that women flatly refuse to wear short skirts for fear of exposing their legs.

October 3, 1900.

Young Wertheimer, the talented son of Ascher Wertheimer, the art dealer of Bond Street, had a Lucullan dinner at his rooms at the Albany last night – all men. Johannes Wolff, the Belgian violinist, Sarasate, Labouchere, straight from the election, young Lord Rosslyn, home from Pretoria after writing a book about it; George Wyndham, statesman, Guardsmen, poet; 'Dolly' Teck, brother of the Duchess of York who will one day be Queen; F. W. Pomeroy, who will one day be a sculptor R. A.; Whistler, looking very fierce, and Sargent, the painter. I drove home to Chelsea with Sargent in a hansom, and he told me that he had not read a newspaper for six months. After dinner, old Ascher, who was beaming, came round and handed us each an enormous cigar, which must have cost him quite two shillings apiece.

Henry Arthur Jones came down this afternoon to tell me that he has hit on a title for his new play. It is *Mrs Dane's Defence*. They have been making a lot of publicity about this secret. Mr Wyndham, Mary Moore, and Lena Ashwell all have fine parts. Jones continues to be the leading dramatist.

People are complaining that the markets are overcharging. I went into Smithfield this morning. They were asking four shillings for long tailed pheasants, which is sixpence more than a year ago, but the market people say there are reasons. No doubt. We also hear of higher rents. Digby, the house-agent, told me that there is a good demand for seven-roomed flats at Ravens Court Park, electric light, all improvements, tennis, no taxes, at £50 to £80 a year. He showed me a sketch of a well-appointed six-room villa at Edmonton at ten shillings a week. I call that reasonable.

I had a whole hour with old Sir Hiram Maxim at lunch today at the Café Royal. The old man drank water and ate some sort of fancy bread that he had in a paper bag. Every now and then he would suck away at a glass contraption which he called his anti-asthma pipe. He said he had spent £17,000 in trying to make a flying machine, but the thing no sooner rose from the ground than it fell down. As for navigable balloons, he agrees with the late Duke of Argyll that man can never overcome the natural laws that condemn all buoyant bodies to an inertia that makes them useless. He does not think Count Zeppelin will have much success with his forthcoming experiments. Maxim gets pink in the face when you mention his brother Hudson. 'He never invented anything,' says the great man, 'except a new powder which blew his arm off. He's trading on my name.'

October 5, 1900.

I went yesterday to Bermondsey to hear young Winston Churchill speak after his Tory victory at Oldham. He spoke in support of Harry Cust, late editor of the *Pall Mall*. Churchill is tall and slight, with brown curly hair, and a boyish face. He simply radiates self-confidence. He began in the true Randolphian style, and at once started to lecture his audience, which was inclined to be enthusiastic. He likened the Liberal Party to the hornet; with the head biting the tail, and the tail stinging the head. The brains of the Liberal Party were all in the tail. He was getting on quite nicely in a speech, half his father and half debating society, when a woman interrupted him, and he lost his temper. Then he said he never was in favour of women's suffrage, and the woman's questions proved that women should not be entrusted with the vote. Someone booed him, and he again lost his temper, talked about 'Yahoos', and said it was more dangerous to face pro-Boers than Boers. Mr Churchill will, in time, acquire the habit of disarming interrupters with a smile. He is still new at the game, but from what I saw of him I think he will never be content to be a back-bencher.

These Post Office people are very conservative. I heard Sir William Preece, the chief engineer of the Post Office, deliver himself today of an unequivocal statement that 'wireless telegraphy is not, and cannot be, a commercial success.' In spite of the delicate and interesting experiments of young Marconi, who is half Italian and half Irish, Preece held that wireless telegraphy cannot supersede the present wire system. 'It may be used under exceptional circumstances by the Army and Navy, but commercially it is impossible.'

Major Arthur Griffiths, who has been governor of Wormwood Scrubs, came down to tell me the news of Pall Mall. He knows all the Army secrets, and has a lot of information, both social and political, while his wife, Kate Reilly, the Mayfair dressmaker, keeps him in touch with affairs feminine. He says that Lieut.-Colonel Plumer, of Rhodesian fame, is to be made a brigadier-general in to-night's Gazette. 'But,' says Griffiths, 'since he is an infantryman and not in the hierarchy he'll go no further.'

Lord Iveagh, the great Irish brewer, is authority for the statement that women clerks in offices are a great success.

He recently tried the experiment of employing lady clerks on the staff of the Guinness Brewery, mostly daughters of employees, and there has been not a single failure.

October 6, 1900.

General election and shooting season have combined to keep people out of town more than usual at this time of year. But Bond Street is beginning to fill again. Gilbert Parker, the novelist, whom I met in Bond Street, had just come up after winning Gravesend for the Tories. He defeated young Hildebrand Harmsworth, Alfred's brother, who had high hopes of success. Mr Parker [now the Rt. Hon. Sir Gilbert Parker, Bart] is quite the most immaculately dressed man in town. He now affects a beard and wears soft silk shirts, even in that temple of sartorial perfection, the House of Commons. I hear his book royalties are £7,000 a year, and perhaps more.

The Liberals are terribly upset at the defeat of Captain Hedworth Lambton, who did such fine work with the naval brigade at Ladysmith. Newcastle has rejected him in spite of his fine war service; but then 'Khaki' wins anything now. Captain Lambton wanted very much to go into Parliament, but he will probably have to be content to go to sea again and wait until he retires as a rear-admiral or the war is forgotten, when, I am told, he proposes to try again.

Yerkes, the projector of the new Charing Cross, Euston, and Hampstead electric underground, for which he has a charter, said to me that in spite of the opposition which he meets at every turn he proposes to go through with it. He has secured the backing of some large American financiers to the extent of £30 million, and he predicted to me that a generation hence London will be completely transformed; that people will think nothing of living twenty or more miles from town, owing to electrified trains. He also thinks that the horse omnibus is doomed. Twenty years hence, he says, there will be no horse omnibuses in London. Although he is a very shrewd man, I think he is a good deal of a dreamer. Yerkes also told me that he had just purchased a Velasquez for his private gallery. He buys paintings without regard to cost. I drove from Westminster with him in his private hansom.

One of the Bass people whom I met this morning gave me the interesting information that breweries are enormously on the decrease. Twenty years ago, in 1880, there were 22,000 brewers; now they number 7,000. In 1882 there were 110,000 private brewers; now there are only 13,000. 'Death by strangulation through the "Tied" system' is the verdict.

Hichens, the manager of the Empire, told me that the music halls are going to suffer if they continue to put on short plays. 'Look at Tivoli', he said, 'always crowded because they stick to their last. This week they have on the bill such favourites as Vesta Tilley, Vesta Victoria, Dan Leno, R. G. Knowles, George Robey, and Harry Lauder. No plays for them.' At lunch today, Romano, the restaurant man, said that claret is becoming almost as cheap as beer. There has been a great vintage of red wines in France, and Romano says all sorts of people are beginning to drink wine. He asserts, too, that sherry is going out rapidly and port as an after-dinner drink is becoming more general. My lunch of four courses, with a bottle of Pommard – there were two of us – cost ten shillings; which for Romano's is not very dear.

October 7, 1900.

Quite a fair assemblage of people in the Church parade in the Row today, in spite of the cold wind. Lord William Beresford, VC, with his rich American wife, who was Mrs Hammersley and afterwards Duchess of Marlborough [stepmother of the present duke], explained the reasons for the failure of his fine colt Volodyovski. He had some fine offers for it, particularly from James R. Keene, the father of Foxhall Keene, the young polo player, who comes to London from New York every season.

A good many politicians in the Park home from the elections. Mitchell-Thomson [father of the recent Postmaster-General] introduced me to Mr A. B. Law [Bonar Law], the new MP for the Blackfriars Division of Glasgow, a Canadian who is in the metal business in Scotland. He says this is his first plunge into political life. A quiet, unassuming man, with no trace of a transatlantic accent, Mitchell-Thomson says he is a mountain of common sense, with an uncanny genius for facts and figures, and that he is a most convincing speaker.

Mrs Williamson, who edits the *Onlooker*, a society gossip paper, had all the women in the Row staring at her. She had some sort of contraption hooked to her skirt to hold it up, thus freeing her hands. She explained that the necessity for holding up the present day long skirts affected the wrist. 'I know many women,' she said, 'who suffer from "skirt wrist."'

The C. I. D. people are busy trying to unearth the gang who gild sixpences to look like half-sovereigns. There has been a flood of them. Inspector Froest, who was in the Park, showed me a handful of them, and Pinkerton, the American detective, who is here, thinks he knows the criminals. Half-sovereigns are becoming unpopular. Only the other night I gave a cabman two sixpences for his fare from Waterloo Place to Fleet Street, and I found later that one of them was half a sovereign. This is a common error when it is dark.

Mark Twain, who has been living at Dollis Hill for some months, sails this week for New York. He was buying books at Hatchard's yesterday, and entertained me with yarns for twenty minutes. 'I always like to spend time in bookshops', he said, 'because it reminds me of my folly in having tried to be a publisher. I lost £20,000 in Webster and Co., and that was a good but costly lesson. I went completely broke.'

He said that the most interesting thing he had found here was that English lumbago was no different from American lumbago. Also that English green cigars are a delusion and a snare. 'I once smoked a piece of bamboo from an old umbrella rib', he said. 'Same thing as English green cigars.'

October 8, 1900.

Swift MacNeill, the pro-Boer, is in again for South Donegal; Lloyd George, ditto, has increased his small majority at Carnarvon by 102. He is thirty-seven years old, but as he is all nerves and jumps, I doubt if he will stand the racket of Parliamentary life for long. He has already been eight years at Westminster, and as he is a turbulent sort of person he is sure to wear himself out soon.

Joe Lyons, who got Salmon and Gluckstein to embark on his catering business, which is now an undoubted success, has asked me to lunch with him at the opening of the new palatial restaurant which his firm has built in Throgmorton Street, by the Stock Exchange. He says you will get a cut off the joint for tenpence the same as at any other City restaurant. Joe spends his time between discussing new palaces and painting landscapes. He might have become an R. A.

The Secretary of the Board of Trade, Mr Llewellyn Smith, is responsible for the statement today that the rise in miners' wages is phenomenal. They have gone up in the past eight months of this year more than twice as much as in the whole of last year. Iron and steel, too, are booming, and wages are going up. But there cannot always be such a great demand for coal, and when the wages come down there must be trouble.

The Rothschild goat, which ambles up and down Piccadilly every afternoon from Seamore Place to Stratford Street, nearly came to grief today. An omnibus horse slipped on the pavement and went down. The goat shied away and was nearly run over by a passing hansom. The omnibus-driver said he wouldn't have hurt the goat for worlds since it might affect the annual New Year's gift of a brace of pheasants which Leopold Rothschild sends to every driver and conductor.

The Rothschild goat is becoming as familiar to London as the chinaware parrot in the window of the Baroness Burdett Coutts at Stratford Street; and apropos of this I note that the baroness, who is just eighty-six this week, is said to have given away a million to charity. Her husband, who was Ashmead-Bartlett, son of a Princeton, New Jersey, professor, and brother of Sir Ellis Ashmead-Bartlett [father of the present Ellis], acted originally as her almoner. Then she married him; and Queen Victoria, her old friend, was very angry because of the disparity in ages. The baroness was about sixty-five when she was married.

Mr Paul Vogel, the secretary of the Waiters' Union, came down to see me to explain that the agitation by the waiters in Trafalgar Square was justified. They have to work from 100 to 115 hours a week 'for disgraceful wages, and are generally treated like dogs.' They have also to hand over a proportion of their tips to the proprietors. Of course, he said, there are exceptions. The meeting was addressed by the inevitable Tom Mann, the publican, who urged them to combine 'for the international solidarity of labour.'

October 9, 1900.

One of the reporters who went to Marlborough House this morning for the departure of the Prince of Wales for Newmarket says that H. R. H. looked very tired and old. He wore a remarkable suit of tweeds and a flaming scarf. He walked out of the gate, shook hands with a police inspector, and then crossed with 'Monty' Guest, his friend, to the Marlborough Club. Then he came out and entered a brougham and drove off to the station with Commander

Seymour Fortescue. The Prince has been visiting Queen
Victoria at Balmoral, and shooting with Lord Glenesk,
of the *Morning Post*, at Glenmuick, where some of the
guests were Sir Donald Mackenzie Wallace, Lady Kilmorey,
Mrs Hope Vere, Mr Arnold Morley, Mrs George Keppel,
and the Grand Duke Michael and Countess Torby.

I had a call from Charles Frohman, the theatrical
impresario, who will soon own half the theatres in New
York and London. He always comes to see me when he is
in London, and we talk over the old days when he was an
advance agent for Haverly's Minstrels in America years ago.
I first saw him sticking bills on the wall of my father's
newspaper building somewhere in the seventies.

The luckiest man in London is 'Tommy Dewar' [now
Lord Dewar], who has won St George's-in-the-East by a
record majority, and all through a horse. He has told me
the secret. He had not a chance when he was adopted on
short notice. Straus, the Liberal candidate, wagered him
four to one on himself. One day last week a deputation
of four men, representing Tower Hamlets costers, waited
on Dewar. They were all dressed up in their best clothes,
covered from head to foot with pearlies. They were not
interested in aliens or deceased wife's sisters, but wanted
to know if Dewar's horse, Forfarshire, had a chance to win
a good race at Newmarket. Dewar, being a Scot, was wary.
He lectured them on gambling, but they persisted. Finally,
in desperation, he gave way, and, pledging them to secrecy,
tipped Forfarshire to win. The next day his agent said that
the whole constituency was on Forfarshire. The costers had
spread the tip, and Dewar was in despair. He was not at
all sure of the horse, and if he lost, his chances of election
were worse than ever. Finally, on Thursday, after a fever of
anxiety – Dewar was afraid to open the telegram – the horse
won by four lengths, and on Saturday Mr. Thomas Dewar
was enthusiastically elected.

The publishers say that Mr Kipling's new book, which is to be called *Kim of Rishti*, will run to a full 100,000 words, which will make a good, thick book. It ought to settle the question whether Kipling is capable of writing other than short stories, since many think that *Captains Courageous* was not a good test. His father, Lockwood Kipling, has done the illustrations as usual.

Very warm today; like midsummer. The thermometer outside my window at noon was seventy-five in the shade. I remember nothing like this in London for years. All the shop windows are full of winter furs.

October 10, 1900.

Six of the Hanoverian cream horses which pull Her Majesty's State coach were out in the Mall this morning drawing a brake. They had their out-riders up, and were evidently practising for the reception, which Queen Victoria proposes to give to the City Imperial Volunteers on their return from South Africa in ten days. The Queen is coming back to town for a few days. She dislikes London and Buckingham Palace, which is becoming very shabby. I am told that Ministers in attendance at Balmoral have been put to some heavy cross-examination by Her Majesty on the question of Kruger's escape from the Transvaal. The old Boer is sure to have a triumphant reception in France this month.

Prison management is becoming enlightened. Mr Troup, at the Home Office, told me today that convicts are now permitted to retain photographs of their relatives in their cells.

A strange luncheon party at the Constitutional Club today. Alfred Jones, the Liverpool ship owner (Elder Dempster), had his weekly assembly of all sorts, about a dozen, each in a different line of business, and he switched off from one to the other on completely different subjects with great facility. He told us that in future everybody would have to eat bananas, for he has arranged to run fast steamers to and from Jamaica, and they will come back packed with bananas. 'I'm going to have them sold off barrows', says Jones, 'and people will become accustomed to them. It will be a bad day for the little Canary Islands bananas, which now come wrapped in cotton wool, and are only seen in shop windows and at dinner parties.'

My tailor, old X——, in Hanover Square, had the telephone put in last week. So today I gave him a great shock. I rang him up and asked him to send me my bill. 'I hope there's nothing wrong', he faltered. 'Nothing', I said, 'except that you have not sent me my bill for a year, and I want to settle up.' 'But, sir', he pleaded, 'I'm sure–' I hung up the receiver. It must have worried him terribly, for he came down to Fleet Street this afternoon, looking like a duke, and begged me to tell him what was wrong, and he hoped I was not leaving him. I could not satisfy him that all I wanted was my bill. He went away quite unhappy at my idiosyncrasy. He can do with long credits, for he charges six guineas for a lounge suit and thirty-five shillings for extra trousers; which, even for Hanover Square, is none too cheap.

October 12, 1900.

I had lunch today in Berkeley Square at Alfred Harmsworth's [afterwards Viscount Northcliffe]. Mr Joseph Choate, the American Ambassador, was there, and we discussed rich men. He said Andrew Carnegie was worth probably from £15 million to £20 million and Rockefeller, of the Standard Oil, probably as much. Harmsworth thought the Czar of Russia was richer, and he believed Cecil Rhodes would one day be the greatest Croesus of all, since his development of the great territories in Africa was bound to pour millions into his pocket no matter how extravagant he might be. Hugh Spottiswoode, the Queen's printer, who was also present, said Morrison, the

City financier, an unknown man, whose name was unfamiliar to all of us, was probably richer in solid money than any of these. [Morrison eventually left ten million.] Kennedy Jones, Mio is a partner of Harmsworth's, and whom I knew in 1890 as a poor reporter, on very small par, stated that in his opinion Whitaker Wright, the great company promoter, was likely to prove wealthier than all the others.

One of the actresses at the Criterion last night wore a pair of white stockings in the new fashion that the French have been vainly attempting to establish this year. Women tell me they will never give up black stockings, which suit them so well. They do not mind the open-work or the daintily embroidered black, preferably silk, but black it must be unless it be brown, and then only with tan shoes.

Captain 'Tucker' Gray, of the 87th (Royal Irish Fusiliers), who is an adjutant of Volunteers [now Territorials] at Hounslow, came in to see me at home this morning, minus his moustache. I expressed surprise at an Army officer in this disguise, and he showed me a letter from his brigadier calling attention to the breach of the rule which requires moustaches to be worn. The brigadier added, 'I don't think it is nice for officers to go about looking like actors.' He has started growing it again, unlike Captain 'Roddy' Owen, who won the Grand National. Owen shaved his moustache, and was ordered not to appear again 'moustacheless' on parade, so the next day he rode out in front of his squadron decorated with an enormous false red moustache like a fox's brush.

At the Café Royal the old lady is talking about removing the red plush lounges and replacing them with chairs; which will be bad, for the charm of this place has been its foreign aspect. One misses the French refugees, such as old Henri Rochefort, who used to come in every afternoon and write his leader for *L'Intransigeant,* and then send it across the street to be telegraphed to Paris. When M. Nicoll presided, there was always a coterie of celebrities like Oscar Wilde,

Whistler, Sir Arthur Sullivan, and George Augustus Sala. I was discussing this today with Charlie Mitchell, whose fight with John L. Sullivan I witnessed at Chantilly a dozen years ago. He and Eugene Stratton, the minstrel who sings negro songs across the way in Prince's Hall, at Moore and Burgess' Minstrels (his real name is Ruhlman), were sipping absinthe and lamenting the falling away of the literary and artistic element from the red benches! Stratton says that 'Pony' Moore, the old minstrel, is now over eighty, but is still hearty in the Finchley Road, where he keeps a private bar in his house free to all visitors.

October 13, 1900.

On the box seat of a Hampstead-bound Atlas omnibus today the old driver was lamenting the fact that so many good horses have been taken away for the war, and that there is no joy in driving the indifferent cattle which now draw the omnibuses. He says his regular box seat customers, who pay a tip of a shilling a week for a reserved seat beside him, are falling away. The young men prefer bicycles nowadays, or hansoms, and the old men do not like climbing up and down now that the omnibuses are so much larger.

The result of Captain Elliot Cairnes' exposures of the ignorance of Army officers in the profession of arms, which has been so apparent in South Africa, is found in the new order, which provides more educational work and less play on the part of officers. The whole system is to be revised and there will be some drastic weeding out of incompetents. The War Office in Pall Mall is, I hear, soon to be torn down, and will remove to the new building in Whitehall. [The Automobile Club stands there now.] Sir Ralph Knox told me today that they are now devoting themselves seriously to the practical consideration of the use of auto-cars in warfare. Lord Roberts is behind this from his experience in South Africa.

I had a note today from my old chief, James Gordon Bennett, of the *New York Herald*, asking me to meet him at the St James's Hotel [now Berkeley], so I went to see him. He was enthusiastic about a new yacht of 1,500 tons, which is to put the proposed new yacht of Joseph Pulitzer in the shade. Anything that Pulitzer, of the *World*, does, stirs Bennett to rivalry. Bennett is going to have all his lights in the form of owls' heads (his motto is '*La nuit porte conseil*' the night brings counsel), and there will be a sea going cow. He also said that he had ordered a 50-horse-power Napier automobile, and that Charles Rolls, S. F, Edge, Lord Carnarvon, Mark Mayhew, and Count Zborowski [the elder] had done likewise. What they will do with these monsters in England I do not know, for they will not be permitted to go beyond the twelve-mile limit.

I asked Moss, the music-hall impresario, if it was true that he is heading a group of managers to check the high salaries now demanded by music hall stars. He denied it, and said that though salaries were too high they have to be paid. Ada Reeve, for instance, receives as much as £150 a week.

October 14, 1900.

The fashion writers in the office are agitated about the suggestion that women's skirts should be shorter. They have gone about interviewing the managers of the great shops, and they are all against it. I have received a note from Paquin on this subject to the effect that short skirts are 'ungraceful and unbecoming, and so distinctly inconvenient.' He says that the skirt two inches off the ground is all right for dry weather, as it leaves both hands free, but not so in muddy weather. Dare to leave it alone and it hangs full and heavy at the back, gathers in all the rain and mud, sweeping wet and uncomfortable round the ankles. Attempt to hold it up and it is too short to reach with any comfort, and becomes most tiring with the twist and drag of it, whereas a really long skirt is lightly thrown over the wrist or arm, and gives no further trouble. The short skirt, to be safely left alone in muddy weather, says this fashion dictator, needs to be at least six inches off the ground; and who dares to wear it!

At the Savoy today little Tod Sloan, the American jockey, who introduced the new style of crouching in the saddle, had a large luncheon party of all sorts. He deports himself like a plutocrat, which he probably is, for he has made a great deal of money, most of which, I am told, he puts away. These American jockeys, Sloan and John and Lester Reiff, manage to lead most of their British colleagues in winning mounts.

The German newspapers continue to fan the anti-British flame in Berlin. Every surrender of five or six Yeomanry is heralded as a great Boer victory, and the newspaper offices, where war bulletins are displayed, have great cheering crowds in front of their windows. I asked Baron Eckhardstein, the counsellor of the German Embassy, today, why their newspapers carry on this pernicious propaganda. He said it was difficult to stop it; that the Emperor was most friendly, and that, after all, reports of pro-Boer feeling in Germany were exaggerated. From what I know of the iron hand of the German Government on its Press, I am not convinced by the baron's explanation. He was rather nervous about it, and appeared to be anxious to show that Germany was really pro-British, which she is not.

Housewives are complaining that the General Election is interfering with game shooting so much that game has become dear. Grouse and partridge are four shillings a brace, old birds 2s 6d a brace, widgeon cost is 6d apiece, and wild duck is 9d to 2s. Fish, however, is quite cheap. Fine soles are 1s 4d a pound, cod and haddock 6d Tomatoes are 4d a pound.

Dr Conan Doyle, who has done fine work with the ambulances in South Africa, is consumed with wrath at his defeat in the Edinburgh election. He was going strong when some Radical enemy put out a poster saying that 'Conan Doyle is a Roman Catholic and a Jesuit. He wants to undermine the Church of Scotland.' That did it.

October 15, 1900.

As I came through the Temple this afternoon I met Mr. Haldane, QC, who has just been returned as a Liberal for Haddingtonshire. He was described yesterday by a fellow-barrister as 'that distressingly respectable young man from Scotland.' He is said to be a most effective pleader at the Parliamentary bar, but there is too much of the dry-as-dust lawyer about him ever to make him popular as a politician. [The late Viscount Haldane, ex-Lord Chancellor.]

The gossips say that Sir Michael Hicks-Beach, 'Black Michael,' is about to retire from the Cabinet. He has been a great success as Chancellor, but his eyesight is troubling him and his temper is becoming worse than ever. I had occasion to go to him with a delegation some months ago, and he treated us like boys and interrupted every one with a short and sharp, 'Well, get on with it', or I know all about that, go on.'

The old Duchess of Devonshire, the 'double duchess', who is a most assiduous whist player, is ill again, and I have arranged to have her obituary notice brought up to date in case of emergency. She has come to Devonshire House from the country. She is a wonderful old woman, who rules her set with a heavy hand. With Lady Londonderry, the Duchess of Portland and the Marchioness of Lansdowne, she has led social England without question. Sir Henry Calcraft, who ran the Board of Trade for years as permanent secretary, told me that he knew her well when she first came to London some forty years ago as the beautiful and accomplished, but poor, daughter of Count von Alten, a Hanoverian soldier who was attached to one of the German legations here. When she married Lord Mandeville, afterwards Duke of Manchester, she was one of the most popular girls in London. She married her second duke, still a bachelor, about nine years ago, after a devoted friendship covering a period of many years since they were young.

London keeps on growing. Today's figures of population are surprising. The Metropolis has 4,210,000 people, which is almost a million more than ten years ago. The expansion to the north and west is rapid. New streets everywhere. The Cricklewood neighbourhood, for instance, will soon lose its sylvan aspect. You cannot now ride cross-country at Finchley with any ease. Everybody wants to come to London; and little wonder, since the rural districts are all more or less dead, with no prospect of revival.

A characteristic note from Charles Wamerv who never appears to grow older, thus, 'Come down this week to the Britannia Theatre, Hoxton, and see your old friend Charles Warner, the celebrated actor, in his so many thousandth appearance as Coupeau in Charles Reade's *Moral Drama Drink*, with all the original effects, fight with real water, realistic scaffold accident, etc. And we conclude with "*Slasher and Crasher*," which will amuse you. George Alexander and W. H. Vernon both came one day last week. I let myself go for them and they both say they were thrilled.'

October 16, 1900.

Alfred Harmsworth [afterwards Viscount Northcliffe] came into my room at the *Daily Mail* office a couple of days ago [this was before I came to the *Daily Express*] and said, 'There is nothing I would like better in all the world than to obtain control of *The Times*. I do not think they are getting on too well over there, and they might like to sell. If I went to them they would at once refuse me. Will you make them an offer instead? You know the Walters, and they may care to deal with you. I've got a million pounds in Consols, and I authorise you to play up to that sum. It will be a great coup if you can get it.' So I went to Printing House Square and saw Mr Godfrey Walter, with whom I had done considerable business in the past in the way of new typesetting machinery, and without beating about the bush made him an offer for control of *The Times*. He looked, and was surprised. I told him to consult his brother Arthur, the senior member of the family, and he agreed to let me know. As I went out he said somewhat naively, 'You are now associated with Harmsworth, aren't you?' I did not deny the soft impeachment. This afternoon I received a nice note from Mr Godfrey Walter, saying he had discussed the matter of my visit in the proper quarter, and he regretted, etcetera. Alfred Harmsworth is disappointed, but he says: 'Never mind. We'll get it sooner or later.'

My cab came down on the slippery pavement of St James' Street today, and I cut my hand in the broken glass of the front. This street is perhaps the most dangerous in London, for it is very steep, and when it rains there is no foothold for the poor horses. Old cabmen avoid it when they can. The trouble is accentuated by the fact that the street is only sanded occasionally when there are royal processions or outings. Otherwise, unlike the other main thoroughfares, no sand or gravel is ever spread on its slippery surface. Sir Eyre Massey Shaw, the ex-chief of the Fire Brigade – 'Oh, Captain Shaw', of the 'cold cascade' – vide, Gilbert and Sullivan – had a bad tumble in a hansom on Saturday in front of Boodle's. Fortunately the window was up, or he would have been badly cut.

October 17, 1900.

Mr W. T. Stead came back from Paris today, and called to say that he had been terribly maligned in a flood of letters and postcards from people who protest against his utterances at a peace meeting in Paris, where he is reported to have said that he was ashamed of being an Englishman. He was particularly hurt at a remark of Sir John Gorst's, that most Englishmen were of a similar opinion since they, too, were ashamed that he was an Englishman. Stead was buzzing away with a full-speed-ahead idea of a newspaper that he would like to found with the object of combating militarism, and to have all the nations united on this policy. But he is afraid the blood lust in nations is too strong for him. A most amiable idealist.

Clement Scott, autocrat of the theatres for a generation, the man who has made and unmade theatrical reputations with a few lines in the *Daily Telegraph,* showed me the prospectus for his new paper, which he has registered at Somerset House as 'Free Lance, Limited.' The capital is £50,000, which shows that Scott means business. He proposes to buy the best talent, and from what I know of this energetic man he will make deep inroads in the circulations of *Truth* and *Vanity Fair* and the *World*. It will probably be a great and lasting success.

Wilson Barrett, the actor, who has a voice like an oboe, was in town today, after a strenuous week at Nottingham, where, he says, the gallery annoyed him every night with cat-calls. He was playing 'Quo Vadis'. On Saturday night, he says, he went before the curtain and gave Nottingham a bit of his mind. He told the audience that Nottingham was a byword with great artists like himself, owing to the incessant interruptions. 'The next time I go to Nottingham', he says, 'I shall play behind a net like the late James Owen O'Connor, the Shakespearean "actor", and so avoid the inevitable shower of oranges and eggs.'

A strange sight at the corner of Piccadilly and Bond Street. There, before the entire world, was 'Joe' Chamberlain leaning out of a hansom, talking to Sir Henry Campbell-Bannerman, the Liberal leader. 'C. B.' was shaking his well dressed sides with laughter, and the Colonial Secretary actually smiled. A week ago they were fighting each other in the election like wild cats.

There is not much to laugh about in 'C. B.'s' camp. So far the new House of Commons has 334 Conservatives and sixty-seven Irish Unionists, as against 187 Liberals, seventy-three Nationalists, and nine Parnellites, which makes a substantial Government majority of 132. Liberals are trying a new tack. Mr R. W. Perks, the solicitor [afterward Sir Robert Perks, 'Imperial Perks'], is forming a new Imperial Liberal party, and he has roped in Lord Rosebery, Sir Edward Grey, Mr Asquith, and Sir Henry Fowler.

October 19, 1900.

Coming through Nevill's Court to Shoe Lane after lunch I was stopped by Keir Hardie, the exminer MP, who lives in the little lane now hallowed by memories of Lovelace and Sir Walter Raleigh. Hardie said, 'Come in, I want to show you a great curiosity.' In his nearby rooms the little man produced a paper box from which he drew a dingy old tweed fore-and-aft hat. 'There', he said, holding it up, 'That hat ought to be put away in the South Kensington Museum. It is famous. It's the hat I wore eight years ago, when I first entered the House of Commons. As I walked in, the whole mass of fine old English gentlemen in frock coats and silk hats rose up and yelled at me. One of them reached out to tear the hat from my head, but I held on in spite of them. It was the first time the House had been desecrated sartorially like that. But times are changing. I have since seen Lord Robert Cecil come into the House in a shabby old soft hat much less attractive than my old deerstalker.' Keir Hardie is a strange little, vain little, honest fanatic, and he has great hopes of his Independent Labour Party's future.

Supper last night in Beerbohm Tree's room at the top of Her Majesty's Theatre, in celebration of the successful rehearsals of Stephen Phillips' 'Herod', which promises to be a theatrical sensation at the end of this month. Tree in great anecdotal form. Miss Bateman, Miss Eleanor Calhoun, Miss Maude Jeffreys, and C. W. Somerset, who have parts, were there; also Alfred Rothschild, Paul M. Potter, who adapted '*Trilby*' for the stage, and Clyde Fitch, the American playwright. Stephen Phillips, who was an actor, promises to become the great stage poet of this era.

The Humanitarian League have been sending appeals to the newspapers today asking support for their campaign against the Royal Buckhounds. They are going to call on Lord Salisbury this week and ask him to abolish them. It looks as if this ardent pack will have to go, sooner or later, though Queen Victoria stoutly declines to interfere. But no successor has been appointed to Lord Coventry as master. The Buckhounds have existed since 1366. The mastership used to be hereditary. It was held for nearly 250 years by the family of Brocas, who came from France, and they finally sold it to Sir Lewis Watson, afterwards Lord Rockingham. One of the principal duties of the mastership is to allocate tickets for the royal enclosure at Ascot. The Humanitarian people say that this could just as well be done by the Lord Chamberlain's department and that it is not enough excuse for the torture of stags in Windsor Park.

October 20, 1900.

Colonel French [afterwards Earl of Ypres] who is looked upon as the most energetic cavalry leader in existence – a fitting successor to Sheridan and Longstreet – has now been gazetted a major-general in the Army. He is a local Lieutenant-General in South Africa. His rise to fame is phenomenal. Few people know him in Pall Mall, but the cavalrymen all swear by him as a dare-devil, hard-riding, hard-swearing soldier, with views of his own. The elusive De Wet paid him a high tribute the other day, when he said he always looks to his next day's fodder supply when French is about. I hear there is friction between French and Kitchener and that Lord Roberts is inclined to side against the hero of Khartoum. I heard today at the War Office that there is no truth in the story that Lord Roberts has refused to come home to be Commander-in-Chief unless he has a free hand. He has made no conditions. There is also a strong report that the old Duke of Cambridge, who was deposed by Lord Wolseley five years ago, is trying to have a finger in the pie again.

Telephone message from Oscar Hammerstein, the American opera house builder, wanting a reporter to interview him on the opera. He says he has just seen Patti and offered her a fabulous sum for another – the hundredth – farewell tour, but the old lady is too comfortable at Craig-y-Nos, her Welsh castle, to risk anything like a protracted tour. She says she is tired of 'Home, Sweet Home', which she invariably has to sing as an encore; had to sing it again in London this week. Hammerstein told me yesterday of his Manhatton Opera House venture in 34th Street, New York, which began with opera, changed over to drama with Mrs Bernard Beere in 'As in a Looking Glass', and ended as a music hall and drinking place. 'First', he said, 'it was Meyerbeer. No good. Then it was Bernard Beere. Also no good. Now it is Lager Beer. Great success!'

At Charbonnel's in Bond Street, where the young people go to drink chocolate, I saw old Sir Tatton Sykes with his famous spouse. He was, as usual, bundled up with three greatcoats and a muffler, although it was not cold, and the energetic Jessica, by way of contrast, was content with a big ostrich feather boa over her tightly laced 'tailor-made' costume. Her sylph-like waist must be the envy of many young girls. The old baronet has written a book called *Sidelights on the War*, and her ladyship whispers aside that he knows more about yearlings – he breeds bloodstock at Sledmere – than warfare although he was once a cavalry officer. Sir Tatton owns about 37,000 acres in Yorkshire, and he says that in another generation land will not be worth owning.

October 21, 1900.

Eliza Carter, one of the 'flower girls' who has sat by the fountain in the middle of Piccadilly Circus for many years, has written a letter to Lord Warwick asking him to give her the name of a good solicitor. Lord Warwick has bought a button-hole from her daily for a long time, and this is her excuse for writing. A man stopped at the fountain on Friday and asked her if she was Eliza Carter, and she did not deny it. 'Well,' he said, 'your uncle has died in Texas and has left you a million dollars' – 'I think he said dollars', adds Eliza, 'but he may have said pounds' – 'Give me five pounds', he says, 'and I will collect the will for you.' Then Eliza continues, 'I would not trouble your lordship, but the man showed me a paper all covered with sealing-wax and ribbons, and my name in red ink in big letters and all, and my uncle's name, but I did not know I had him. I have seen too much in Piccadilly in my time to lose my head even over a million, so if your lordship will help me to a good solicitor I'll be obliged to your lordship.'

At the Savage Club I heard two new views of London. Louis Becke, the novelist of the Pacific Ocean, said he felt more lost and lonely in London than he ever did on the loneliest of South Sea Islands, and George Ade, the author of *Fables in Slang*, asserted that Cockney English was the most expressive, the most musical and the most attractively slangy of all the slangy languages in the world. 'How many languages do you know?' asked Weedon Grossmith, the painter-actor, 'None', answered Ade.

Mr Dowie, the American evangelist, tells his audiences that London is the wickedest city the world has ever known, and that it becomes more ribald and drunken every day. He knows nothing about it. I have frequently noticed that London improves year by year. It is a perfect fairyland compared with ten years ago. I remember when Tottenham Court Road and the Strand were impossible after eight p.m. I walked with D'Oyly Carte from the Grand Hotel at Charing Cross at nine o'clock last night (Saturday), as far as Savoy Hill, always the worst part of the Strand. We counted only nine men and five women who were unsteady with drink, and in not one instance were we molested; which shows that London is improving instead of going backward.

Sir Thomas Lipton proposes to have a second try for the America Cup with his yacht Shamrock. I saw him in the Park today with Arbuckle, the American coffee and sugar king. Lipton said *Shamrock* was 'hoodooed' by the Americans. 'They put something in the water so that I could not win.' 'What was it, please?' asked Arbuckle. '*The Columbia*,' answered Sir Thomas, always ready with his little joke.

October 22, 1900.

These cold nights are bad for the outsleepers on the Embankment. There are not enough benches to accommodate the large number of homeless, shivering people. I stopped my cab on my way home early this morning to observe a Salvation Army official who was distributing soup tickets. He told me that his average distribution of tickets on his beat from Blackfriars to Westminster is 200 tickets between midnight and two o'clock, and there is a fair sprinkling of women and children. They would have a terrible time – bad enough as it is – but for the Salvation Army. I do not gain much favour when I proclaim, as I often do, that General Booth is one of the greatest men of the Victorian era.

Carl Haag, the old water-colour painter, who taught Queen Victoria and has made a fortune from his art, informs me that he is going to return to Germany, which he left many years ago, and proposes to end his days in a restored castle on the Rhine. He intends, however, to continue sending his pictures for exhibition at the Water Colour Society. Haag says that in his view the vogue of watercolours has temporarily, at least, come to an end. The new type of houses which are now being built do not lend themselves to mural embellishment, and the rich City merchants who for the past forty years have patronised watercolour art so that it has become as fine as that of the Georgian oil painters, are going in for portraits and coloured mezzotints. 'But,' he says, 'fifty years or so from now the Victorian water colours of today will be in great demand, and the possessors of Herkomers, MacWhirters, Danbys, David Coxs, and Tophams will receive great fortunes for their specimens. They are a splendid "lock-up".'

Charles Wyndham, the actor, and his brother-in-law Bronson Howard, the playwright, who wrote *Brighton*, *The Henrietta*, and *Shenandoah*, were in fine form anecdotally between the acts last night at Wyndham's Theatre. I urged Wyndham to write his experiences as a surgeon in the Northern Army during the American Civil War in the sixties. He told of a surgeon who had an original way of performing operations. There were no anaesthetics. If it was a bad case requiring a quiet patient, the gentle surgeon just hit the victim a tap on the head with an iron bar, knocked him senseless, and then proceeded to cut off his arm or his leg. Sometimes the shock was fatal, but the inventive surgeon maintained that it was generally successful and much kinder, and the operation was more easily conducted.

October 23, 1900.

There is a good opportunity for police interference in Holywell Street, that dingy old Elizabethan thoroughfare with its overhanging fronts, which runs from St. Clement

Danes at the Law Courts, with Wych Street, into the slum district of the Bill Sikes country. I came through there today as far as the old Globe Theatre at Newcastle Street, and its shop windows were besieged by a crowd of clerks in their midday rest hour. These windows and front shelves are packed with vicious and gaudy literature, and other material, whose sort is hardly to be matched in the lowest quarters of Paris. If it were not for the further advertisement that this noxious old street was to receive, and thus increase its clientele, I should expose it in print. There are also one or two shops with good old books. Colonel Howard Vincent, who was head of the C. I. D. at Scotland Yard, says they once tried to clean out the vicious stands, but never succeeded, and now they have given it up because they hope that when the County Council gets to work on its improvements between the Strand and Holborn, Holywell Street and Wych Street must necessarily be included. Norman Shaw, the architect, told me the other day that he had been consulted on the scheme. He wants to make a great boulevard and base it on an ornamental circle opposite Somerset House, but he does not think it will ever come to pass.

Musical comedy has, doubtless, come to stay for a long time, and melodrama, which has now reigned for a generation or two, must take a back seat. Here is George Edwardes announcing the anniversary of *San Toy* at the Gaiety. Who would have dreamed of such a thing ten years ago! Edwardes believes that 'San Toy' is a lucky name. He has named one of his racehorses after it, and I was glad to hear today that the piece has also brought a great deal of money to Edward Morton, its talented author.

The syndicate of London dealers who, through M. Duprez, paid £13,200 to Prince Chigi, of Rome, for the famous Botticelli picture of the Virgin and Child got their prize away just in time. The Italian Government, which prohibits the sale of old masters, was caught napping, but I am informed that

Prince Chigi is to be prosecuted, and if the facts are as stated, he will not only be minus his Botticelli, but the £3,200 as well.

I have just noticed a new form of night advertisement. It consists of boards with prepared surfaces, capable of conducting an electric current. You can arrange any number of letters, attached to the current, and spell out words. They will be useful in front of theatres for, saying 'House Full' and other announcements, and the idea has great possibilities.

October 24, 1900.

Rapid changes are coming over London. By and by there will be no private residences in Piccadilly, where once there were only residences. The transfer of the Isthmian Club from Walsingham House, opposite Devonshire House, to the fine bow-fronted residence of the late Sir Julian Goldsmid, next to the St. James Club, marks another loss of a private mansion. Further up a new imperial service club is soon to occupy No. 110. It has exchanged all the fine old Georgian mahogany furniture with Maple's for modern chests and chairs. If 'Old Q.' (Queensberry) were alive now he would bemoan the coming destruction of his favourite balcony, from which he used to ogle the ladies. The Bath Hotel, beloved of county families, will soon be coming down, and with it will disappear the nightly candles and the tin baths that are carried into bedrooms every morning. There is presently to be a new hotel [the Ritz] to cover the site of the Bath and Walsingham House.

There was a card of invitation this morning for the Automobile Club's run from London to Southsea, on November 10. It promises to be a momentous affair. Over twenty-five vehicles have already been entered. Every effort, say the managers, will be made to ensure an orderly procession, and no car will be permitted to pass the pilot between London and the south side of Esher Hill. The cars will enter Portsmouth in line. Several manufacturing firms are offering seats at a reasonable price, so that those who would like to experience the joys of motoring for the first time may have an excellent opportunity.

Julian Ralph, the famous war correspondent, entertained us in the office today with his recent experiences in Africa. He said, 'If you see dust on the veldt it's smoke; if you see smoke it's dust; if you see smoke low down and high up it's a farm well on fire, so you need not hurry; there is no chance of loot ... If you see a galloping Boer, it's nothing. You never see Boers and they don't gallop. If a trooper brings you specimens of Boer dum-dum bullets that he has picked up on the veldt, don't pay any attention. They are probably used up soda-water Sparklets left behind by one of our officers' messes.'

Had a note this evening from Maida Vale that Robert Buchanan has had a paralytic stroke and is not expected to live. I suppose the old playwright's quarrel with Mrs Langtry over his play '*Marie Antoinette,*' which she bought from him has upset him, since she has now commissioned a Frenchman to write one on the same subject for production at her Imperial Theatre, Westminster. [Now the site of the Wesleyan Central Hall.]

October 26, 1900.

Poor old Sims Reeves is dead at last. The news came in this afternoon and we shall never again hear him sing '*Come into the Garden, Maud.*' I heard him sing it a year or so ago at an Empire matinee. His fine tenor voice was a voice no longer, but he got a great ovation. He began over sixty years ago. Old Colonel Mapleson once told me that as far back as 1847 he heard Reeves sing *Edgardo* in *Lucia di Lammermoor,* 'and believe me or not, I was so affected that I cried.' I was not quite sure how he meant this, but there is no doubt that Sims Reeves was the greatest ballad singer of this century. He had a Civil List pension of £100, and a new wife whom he married five years ago, at the age of seventy-seven. He was taken ill in a provincial hotel. A young girl came in to nurse him, and out of gratitude he married her.

Shopkeepers in the Burlington Arcade are again complaining about the obstruction caused at the Piccadilly entrance by the young bloods from Tufnell Park and Acton and Tooting Bee, who congregate there after five o'clock in the afternoon, all dressed up in frock coats, highly polished hats and lavender gloves. They stand tightly wedged together leaning on their gold and silver-mounted sticks, looking bored and imagine that they give the impression to passers-by that they are all heirs to peerages and great estates and are just out for an airing. This afternoon I saw young X., one of our clerks, in the languid group. Now I know why he is always so anxious to get away before five. A strange fad.

One of Jabez Balfour's white elephants, the Hotel Cecil, which he built with Liberator money, is justifying itself by making profits. I have just had the company's annual report. When the new Strand front is finished it will be one of the finest hotels in Europe. The new front will cost £400,000, and it will replace a lot of ramshackle houses that used to cluster round what, until recently, was Cecil Street.

'Jack' Joel, one of the Barnato firm, made a bet of £25 recently that Mr. George Howard, a stockbroker, weighing 13st. 71b, would carry Mr Douglas MacRae, a City journalist, weighing 13st., one hundred yards in Throgmorton Street. There was, however, such a crowd that the effort was abandoned, but Mr Joel gave a consolation dinner at the Carlton Hotel last night, the like of which has not been served in London since the famous Phillips dinner at the Savoy, when the fruit was served direct from' the trees and the bill was £15 per plate. Mr Joel's was, I hear, £10 each.

October 27, 1900.

Mr Chamberlain has gone for a Mediterranean cruise, accompanied by his son Austen, who is a Civil Lord at the Admiralty. They will arrive today at Marseilles, to go aboard H. M. S. Caesar. By a strange coincidence, Oom Paul Kruger is expected to arrive there today on board the Dutch cruiser Gelderland after his flight from Pretoria. It would be funny if the two protagonists met on 'neutral' ground.

Poor old General George Cox, who walks about London with nothing to do, is a fine example of how the War Office muddled things when the war began. He was a most efficient soldier in command of the troops in Natal, and for three years exercised them and manoeuvred them over all the ground where the first fighting occurred. He knew every yard of the Elandslaagte-Spion-Kop-Ladysmith country. A week before war broke out he was relieved 'on account of age' – he is a little over sixty-one and was ordered home with his staff! Strangers took his place – and Lady-Smith was bottled up. Not once has General Cox been sent for to go to Pall Mall to be consulted and yet he knew all about the country in which so many disasters have occurred in the past ten months.

Enormous crowds in the streets all day expecting the arrival of the City Imperial Volunteers on their return from the war, but they were doomed to disappointment, for the *Aurania* has been detained by fog and did not arrive at Southampton. Much disappointment because the Queen has not come to London from Balmoral to greet them.

I was nearly suffocated today in an Inner Circle steam train between Sloane Square and the Temple. The carriage was filled with sulphurous smoke and my fellow-passengers in the packed compartment coughed incessantly. Some day the electrification plans of this stuffy line may be completed, but in the meantime the smoke nuisance is most trying.

Lord Rosebery, of whom it was said that he has three great achievements to his credit – the Derby, the Premiership, and the richest bride – announces his withdrawal from the Turf. One of his horses, Caterham Lad, sold at Newmarket yesterday for 1,200 guineas and others fetched from 260 guineas upward. The total was 7,295 guineas. Lord Rosebery is busy these days exhorting Londoners to vote in the borough election. He wants the factories to be removed from London and the workers taken with them.

My market report shows that provender is fairly cheap. Pheasants are 6s a brace, hares 4s, larks 2s a dozen, good soles 10d a lb, turbot and brill 6d.

October 28, 1900.

The *Aurania* did not arrive at Southampton with the popular C. I. V.'s until late in the afternoon and so the troops remain on board over Sunday, much to the disappointment of their friends. Colonel Mackinnon, their commander [the late Gen. Sir Henry Mackinnon], says they could have gone into Plymouth if they had known that London was waiting for them with a great reception, and so could have reached here in time, but, of course, they were out of touch with land. The procession will therefore take place tomorrow. There has been no such excitement since Mafeking Day last spring.

I had a call in the morning from Mr W. Broderick Cloete, the landed proprietor and racing man, who is mixed up with South African affairs. He is keen to start a daily paper with the avowed object of promoting the expansion of the Empire, and he wanted my advice and cooperation. 'How much money are you prepared to lose?' I asked. 'Lose?' he cried. 'Nothing. It would be a great success at once.' I explained that it would not be safe to begin without a capital of at least £300,000. 'Well', he replied, 'Harmsworth says he only put down £10,000 for the *Daily Mail* four years ago, and I understand Arthur

Pearson is already making money on the *Daily Express*, so why couldn't I do the same?' I smiled at this, for Pearson is reported to have lost £2,000 a week since he started the *Daily Express* last April. Cloete was most persistent and rather vexed at my refusal to change my views, particularly after I showed him that all the Unionist papers are strongly imperialistic and there is no room for another morning paper.

John Strange Winter (Mrs Stannard), the talented lady who wrote *Booties' Baby*, entertained me for a quarter of an hour on the subject of women's coiffures – most interesting. She says the toupee, or transformation has come to stay. No more disarranged curls, no more frowsy fringes at the damp seaside, and no more lace caps for ladies past fifty. A duplicate transformation makes it possible to dress the hair in two minutes. I learned with astonishment that some women pay as much as thirty pounds for an artistic addition, but that you can get a nice one for from three to five guineas. Also women who suffer from neuralgia – and they nearly all do, owing, I think, to tight lacing – derive great benefit from the transformation; at least Mrs Stannard says so.

A plumber's assistant came yesterday morning to repair a leaking drainpipe. I noticed that he smoked many cigarettes. I mentioned this later to Mayo Gunn, who was manager of the *St James's Gazette*, but has now joined his relatives, the Wills, of Bristol, in the tobacco business. He says workingmen are taking more and more to cigarettes, which are so much cheaper since the introduction of machinery. A man named Bernard Baron [late head of Carreras] brought over a machine a few years ago and he turns out thousands per hour. He is likely to make a fortune.

October 29, 1900.

The scenes in the streets today when the C. I. V.'s marched through the town were astounding. Mile upon mile of cheering crowds. Hooliganism everywhere. Police arrangements hopeless. Two killed and thirteen injured in the crush. Hundreds of lost children. The Prince of Wales [Edward VII] waved his hat at the soldiers from Marlborough House. Lord Wolseley read them a welcoming message from the Queen at the H.A.C. barracks, but before they got there the crowd repeatedly broke up the military formation. The Lord Mayor made them all Freemen of the City. There never was a more mismanaged public procession. London has gone mad again, and tonight there have been the usual scenes in the streets with four-wheelers packed in and out with rollicking youth. Accidents due to horses shying at motor cars are far too frequent. Many motorists refrain from slowing down or stopping their engines when they approach horses on the road. If this precaution were more generally observed there would be fewer accidents. I have just been told of a fatality of this sort on the Brighton Road, in which a woman was killed in a runaway. Sir Walter Gilbey, who drives about the Essex roads in the Stansted district in a phaeton, with outriders, complains bitterly that his horses run great risks whenever a motor comes along. He never drives on the main Cambridge road now for fear of meeting a motorcar.

I have just finished reading *The World's Great Snare*, by Mr E. Phillips Oppenheim, a fine study of stirring times in the Far West. This young author is fast coming forward as a writer of life in the mining camps.

A narrow escape today while crossing Trafalgar Square from being run down by a bicyclist 'scorcher'. The police appear to be incapable of putting an end to this dangerous habit and when the culprits are caught they appear to get off too lightly. Sir Albert de Rutzen, at Bow Street, is one of the few magistrates with a proper sense of punishment fitting the crime. He lets them have it strong.

The Rev. J. M. Bacon, the most daring of ised for aerial transport, but he thinks little of Count Zeppelin's experiments in the air. In his view internal combustion engines are not powerful enough to do the work.

October 30, 1900.

Andrew Carnegie is in town from his Scottish castle for a few days. I went shopping with him today. He wanted some handkerchiefs and a couple of neckties. When we came out he said that London's shopping methods are all wrong. 'Just look at the jumble in the windows', he said. 'So much stuff that you cannot take it all in. And when you go into a shop they treat you most indifferently. You are scowled at if you ask for goods out of the ordinary, and you are made to feel uncomfortable if you do not buy. These shop people drive away more people than they attract. That's all wrong. I'd like to own a big draper's shop in Regent Street. I'd show 'em!' He recurred to this grievance throughout the hour that I was with him. 'What London wants', he said, 'is a good shaking up.' Then he went away to think about giving away some more millions.

Three notable deaths to record. 'Bill' Yardley, the cricketer and critic, who appears in late years to have fallen on evil days; Professor Max Muller, the Oriental scholar of Oxford and friend of Lord Salisbury; and Prince Christian Victor of Schleswig-Holstein, grandson of the Queen, who died of enteric in a military hospital at Pretoria, aged thirty-three. Prince Christian was popular in the Army. The trades people will make their usual complaint against the inevitable mourning order which puts society in black for another term. Queen Victoria insists on Court mourning for all her relatives, and since she is related to most of the reigning houses this comes pretty hard on our fashion providers.

John Morley, who was once editor of the *Mall*, proposes to do a Life of Gladstone which, he says, will be better than his Cromwell. He thinks a journalist's life is to be preferred to any other. He came into the Savoy today accompanied by his secretary, and gave me what he said was Dion Boucicault's advice to journalists from his experience as a popular playwright. Boucicault's views are that there are three guiding principles in stagecraft and journalism, which, if followed, cannot fail to be successful. They are: (1) Money, (2) Love, (3) Stomach. Money interests everybody. Love comes to everybody, and includes envy, hatred, jealousy, loyalty, honour, and all the other human and spiritual attributes. Stomach takes in everything that is physical.

I find that if I wish to lay my hands on any one who is prominent in public or social life I have to send to the Princes' Skating Rink in Knightsbridge. 'Meet me at Princes' is becoming as familiar as 'Meet me at Jimmy's' used to be. The skating vogue, now that it is too cool to lounge in the Park, is quite the thing.

October 31, 1900.

Lunch today in Ridgemount Gardens with Joseph Hatton, perhaps the most prolific writer of the past twenty years. Only last week he finished a book called *In Male Attire*. W. S. Gilbert was there, and he talked a lot about his experiences as a clerk in the Privy Council office forty years ago and his unfulfilled ambitions at the Bar. He thinks Edward Carson [now Lord Carson], who has made a great position at the English Bar since his daring prosecution of Oscar Wilde, is perhaps the most successful man in the Law Courts today, run close by Rufus Isaacs [now Lord Reading], who began life before the mast. Gilbert has made a great deal of money out of his partnership with Sir Arthur Sullivan, and, like most successful men, he ate sparingly and spoke a good deal about his digestion, which I imagine worries him a lot. Most humorists seem to be thus afflicted.

I understand that owing to the terrible confusion at the London docks, which are administered by forty different authorities, the Royal Commission, which has been sitting on this muddle, has decided to recommend a single body to take control. London has lost a great deal of business owing to this dock confusion.

Horace Fletcher, the man who is mostly responsible for the infliction of Japanese fans and other cheap Oriental gewgaws on Europe and America, has developed a new one. Like Luigi Coraaro, the Italian nonagenarian, he has found youth by chewing every morsel of food until it is no longer chewable, and this has reduced Fletcher from fifteen stone to ten stone in weight, and given him the strength and endurance of a young giant. A year ago he was just a fat, flabby, helpless invalid, and we had to assist him into a four-wheeler. Now he rides a bicycle before breakfast for twenty miles and never tires. He came in to see me this evening. Wants me to go to the Paris Exhibition with him, thence to Avignon, Nimes, and Arles, and bicycle from there via Marseilles along the Riviera to Genoa and Venice, where he contemplates buying a palace on the Grand Canal. I shall probably go.

Today marks the end of all the old London vestries, and the new borough councils, with their mayors and maces and councillors come into being. Town hall, not vestry hall, in future, and thirty-odd mayors in procession to represent Greater London. Westminster is now one of the world's greatest cities, but none of them will compare with the splendours of the old City of London, which goes on feasting and wining in its ancient company halls as it has for centuries.

NOVEMBER

November 2, 1900.

The news is out, and official, that Lord Lansdowne is to succeed Lord Salisbury at the Foreign Office. This will provoke a protest from many quarters. Opinion is divided on his capacity, particularly since he has not been a great success at the War Office, where in present circumstances no one could succeed. Sir William Harcourt, who is nothing if not caustic, says that the reason Lord Lansdowne is to go to the Foreign Office, is because he speaks good French and he leaves the War Office because he does not speak the Dutch Taal. Lord Selborne goes to the Admiralty and Mr C. T. Ritchie to the Home Office. Black Michael (Sir M. Hicks Beach) will remain at the Treasury, and George Wyndham goes to Ireland. This young Guardsman poet has come on very fast of late.

The old story of lawyers being careless in the making of their wills is illustrated in the last testament of Lord Russell, of Killowen, the late Lord Chief Justice, who left nearly £150,000, but omitted to initial the codicil; and he was usually an extremely careful man in such matters. It is a coincidence, today, that with the publication of Lord Russell's will comes the sale of Parnell's estate in Ireland, thus once more bringing before the public two great figures in the famous *Times* forgery case.

Old Bullivant, the silk hat ironer at Carter's, in Fleet Street, took a day off yesterday, because it was his birthday. Otherwise, he says, he has not had a holiday for years. He went to Lincoln and Bennett's, in Piccadilly, and spent most of the time watching the hat ironer there, and he tells me he has gained a few new ideas. He says, too, that silk hats are now more worn than ever, and that it is a delight to polish the fashionable hats that cost £1, as against the cheap stuff that the clerks buy in the City at 10s. The nap doesn't last.

Some people carry their prejudices rather far. I sent a reporter today to see a City banker on an important matter. He saw him, but also sent me a note – he is a personal friend – suggesting that in future I might like to take into consideration the fact that reporters should conform to custom by coming into the City attired in a manner more in keeping with the dignity of their calling; meaning that they should not wear bowler hats and brown boots. I have taken the hint and issued an order in accordance with tins rebuke.

November 3, 1900.

Lady Charles Beresford, who knows everything and everybody, told me today that the recent naval battle in the Mediterranean manoeuvres, between the rival squadrons of Lord Charles and Sir J. Fisher [afterwards Lord Fisher of Kilverstone] has left a legacy of considerable bad blood, with no end of recrimination and an official intervention by the Admiralty, which declines to permit the two admirals to carry their quarrel to the state of a public inquiry. Lady Charles also told me a great secret – which everybody knows – namely, that the Marchioness of Bute, with her children, has gone to the Holy Land to bury her late husband's heart on the Mount of Olives. This was Lord Bute's wish; so her goldsmiths have made a beautiful golden casket, in which the heart is deposited, and Lady Bute has carried it all the way to Jerusalem, never losing sight of the precious casket.

I have today received a telegram which I shall keep as a curiosity. It is a wireless message sent to me from the Belgian cross-Channel steamer *Princess Clementine*, between Dover and Ostend. The steamer had a wireless instrument fitted on deck, and left this morning to carry out the experiment, which marks a new era in communication at sea. The British postal authorities are, of course, taking the usual attitude of a mixture of aloofness and opposition. The Marconi people wanted permission to put up a tower at Dover, but this was withheld, and so the message which came today had to come through Belgium. It was flashed from the steamer to Lapanne. Thence it was sent by land telegraph to Brussels and then by land and cable to London. The Post Office attitude reminds me of their decision ten years ago when Mr William Russell inaugurated the messenger callboy service. That was considered to be an infringement of the Postmaster-General's monopoly, and Russell had to pay tribute of a penny for every messenger call. This Marconi experiment today was important. It is not difficult to envisage the possibilities of the new system of communication. Mr Marconi predicts a wide range of ocean telegraphy, even beyond the present 30-mile limit, and we are thus encouraged to believe that many disasters at sea will be prevented.

Edna May, the toast of young London for several years, telephoned this afternoon that Charles Frohman has asked her to return to New York at once to appear in a new comedy. She has made a wonderful success. When she came here in The Belle of New York she had little experience beyond the second row of the chorus, from which George Lederer selected her. I know of no quicker rise in a short time, except that of May Yohe, in her *Honey, my Honey.*

The municipal elections have proved a great success for the Conservatives, who call themselves Moderates. Their figures are 825, as against 455 Progressives and 82 Independents. The fight was against Radicalism and extravagance. Reckless expenditure always occurs when the Radicals have control of other people's money.

November 4, 1900.

Mr Lee, the Court veiler, of Wigmore Street, showed me some of his pet creations in veils for women. He was just packing up a new set for the Empress of Russia, a special design of plain, clear, net, with a chenille spotted edge and worked by hand. English princesses prefer a clear net with small evenly set spots. This spotting is becoming popular. The spots are hand-sewn, and Mr Lee showed me a lot of girls sewing them on. He is especially proud of his popular 'Nell Gwynne' veil, which has only two black velvet 'beauty spots'.

'Monty' Guest, the Prince of Wales's confidant, came down for a Sunday chat. He says H. R. H. is anxious to let us know that he has private information that neither the Kaiser nor the French President intends to give Kruger a reception, and that the Kaiser does not even intend to see him. The situation with the Kaiser is rather delicate. If we admonish him too much he may throw discretion to the winds and receive Kruger merely from pique. Guest did not say so in so many words, but I imagine H. R. H. has been exchanging some rather intimate home truths with his fiery nephew. I think Mr. Guest's visit had a good deal of diplomacy in it, and that he is paving the way to an easier reception for the Kaiser on his threatened visit to his august grandmother at Windsor. Germans have been making a lot of anti-British capital out of the divorce suit which the Princess Aribert of Anhalt (Queen Victoria's granddaughter) has instituted. The German Court says she is ultra-English in her ideas of freedom, but they admit that Prince Aribert is inconsiderate and extravagant.

A letter last night from a farmer, who lives near my weekend cottage in Essex, complaining that I am spoiling the labour market by overpaying my man-of-all-work, who has been heretofore rated as a farm labourer. I pay him eighteen shillings a week, which is more than the regular wage of farm labourers in the district, but then he looks after the garden and airs the cottage. I am trying to buy the place, but since it is copy- hold and not freehold, there are great difficulties. The superior landlord, the agent and the solicitor, all have to be compensated, so that the fines for enfranchisement come to a tidy-proportion of the purchase price. Land, however, is worth only about £7 per acre, and the total will not be great. The present rental for ten acres, with house, is about £28 per year. The copyholder, whose tenant I am, pays to the overlord, who happens to be Lady Warwick, an annual fine of a sheep; at least, he is supposed to render this tribute.

November 5, 1900.

There is to be a determined onslaught on the principle of income tax in the next session by a number of back benchers, among them that effective stump orator, Mr George Doughty, of Grimsby. He told me today that the tax [8d in the £] weighs too heavily on people with moderate incomes, and that it constitutes a hindrance to trade. He saw the Chancellor about it one day last week, and 'Black Michael' retorted characteristically, 'You ought to be damned glad it isn't tenpence in the pound!' The Revenue people have recently made it rather unpleasant for people who are a year behind in their payments.

The motor-car built for the Prince of Wales was being driven all the way to Sandringham on Saturday, and at Finchley one of its tyres collapsed. The driver, wearing the royal uniform, had the car hauled to a local cycle shop, where it was repaired, and the journey continued.

That irrepressible letter writer, Mr Algernon Ashton, who never fails to put forward a new topic for public discussion, or discover a decayed tombstone, sends me a line asking for publicity on the subject of Bulwer Lytton's birthplace, at 31, Baker Street. He wants the Society of Arts to put up a tablet in commemoration.

Mr. Hanbury looks like going to the Treasury as Financial Secretary. He is very rich, but an ambitious politician. He told me the other day of a coal mine – he is a coalowner – in Wales, which pays 130 per cent., and another in Northumberland paying 105 per cent, which shows that coal mining is a fine thing. Hanbury also told me the secret of Lord Beauchamp's resignation of the governorship of New South Wales. When Lord Hopetoun was made Governor-General of the new Commonwealth, Sir William Lyne, the Premier of N. S. W., told Lord Beauchamp that the people expected him to give up Government House in the new Governor-General's favour. There is as yet no provision for a Commonwealth palace, but Lord Beauchamp declined. He offered, however, to entertain the Earl of Hopetoun and staff at Government House at his own expense. 'Bill' Lyne would not have this, so Lord Beauchamp made up his mind to resign, and he is coming home.

I held the stake today, £5 a-side, in a wager between Monsieur Van Branteghem, that strange little Belgian diplomat-financier, who wears a golden bracelet, a gold-rimmed monocle, and an enormous gold watch chain, and Marcus Mayer, who was Patti's manager for many years. The bet was that Van Branteghem could walk all the way on the kerb side of Regent Street from Verrey's to Piccadilly and that he would not have more than three mud splashes from passing horses' hoofs on his collar. When we reached Swan and Edgar's corner the little Belgian had five blobs on his high collar and three for luck on his face.

Today was Guy Fawkes' Day. I have never seen so many guys in the streets.

November 6, 1900.

I hear authoritatively that Lord Stanley, MP [now Lord Derby], is to have office as Financial Secretary to the War Office, and that his appointment is to be made in a day or two. He has been a most zealous and rather rigid Press censor in South Africa, and some of the correspondents have complained bitterly of his official attitude, though personally he is always amiable. Being the son of the Earl of Derby, he is naturally in the running for preferment. I hear, too, that Lord Salisbury has offered the Local Government Board to Mr Walter Long, now President of the Board of Agriculture, of whom it is said that when the Prime Minister met him recently and shook hands, Lord Salisbury turned afterwards to Mr Arthur Balfour and asked, 'Who is that rather pleasant man?' Mr Balfour is even more absent-minded than his distinguished uncle, and he is reported to have said, 'I know his face very well, but I cannot remember his name. But I think he is one of your Ministers.' Rather rough on the man who stamped out rabies from these islands.

The Home Office appears to be alarmed about our rapid consumption of coal. The report they send down today states that we are producing twice as much as we did thirty years ago and five times more than fifty years ago. The total output for last year was more than 220 millions tons. There will be a serious coal famine soon within the lives of the present generation unless we exercise economy.

Colonel 'Bill' Carington [Equerry to the Queen], at the Café Royal today, stated that when the Duke and Duchess of York [King George and Queen Mary] go on their Australian tour early in the year they will sail in a mail steamer, and not on board a man-of-war. The Australian liners are growing in size; one or two of ten or twelve thousand tons. Mail steamers generally are becoming larger. The Germans are talking of a ship of 30,000 tons, which beats the *Oceanic* and the *Celtic*. They register about 20,000 tons or so, which is double the size of ten years ago.

Mrs Rendle and Miss Tattershall write from Baker Street that they have opened a new tea room, in which there are to be found lady proprietors, lady waitresses in pretty frocks, and ladies to bake the cakes, pastries, and scones, and where the walls are decorated with attractive pictures and hangings, and so on. The new woman progresses.

November 7, 1900.

James McNeil Whistler was over from Paris today and holding forth as usual. His latest grievance is that Yerkes proposes to put up a gigantic powerhouse in Chelsea for the electrification of the Underground, and as it is to have enormous chimneys towering far into the sky, it will completely ruin the bend of the Thames made famous by Turner. 'They ought to be drawn and quartered', says the author of Gentle Art of Making Enemies. Whistler had on a soft hat, and for once he had discarded his flowing tie. 'I used to wear the tie' he said, 'when there were artists in the world. There are none now.'

Considerable agitation among City councillors and tradesmen, led by Lord Mayor-elect Green, against the congestion of street traffic, particularly in the mornings, when the main thoroughfares are packed with heavy goods vans that block up the roadways and make progress difficult. Mr. Deputy Weingott, who is active in the protest, said today that if this congestion of traffic continues London will be impossible in five years. It is obvious that this will be the case unless the authorities provide one or two new streets leading to and from the City.

An amusing half-hour with Jim O'Kelly, MP, the most romantic figure in Parliament. He stuck to Parnell to the last, and told me many humorous stories of Parnell's iron hand and the humility of the otherwise turbulent Home Rule members whenever they were in his presence.

O'Kelly's experiences in the Carlist revolution and in the Franco-Prussian War are described by him in a masterly way; and his story of how he ensured the safety of the Empress of Mexico on her flight from the rebels who executed her husband, Maximilian, would read like a romance by Dumas. The Law Society is agitated about the increase of defalcations among solicitors who make free with their clients' money.

The arrest of Benjamin Lake, ex-chairman of the Society's Discipline Committee, who is involved in enormous losses, has brought the matter to a climax, and there will probably be new legislation. The worst feature of these many defalcations is that so many trust funds of infants are involved, and some method must be devised, preferably under Government control, to protect them. The temptations to otherwise responsible men are very great. Unlucky speculation appears to be the principal cause of ruin.

November 9, 1900.

The new Lord Mayor, with his show, had the day to himself. It was partly military and partly Drury Lane. I liked the keepers of the Epping Forest in their uniforms, and the crowd was enthusiastic over the 4in. gun of the cruiser *Powerful* (imitation it was), which Captain Percy Scott's sailors carried to Ladysmith on the improvised gun carriage. At the Law Courts Lord Alverstone (Sir Richard Webster) the new Lord Chief Justice, did the honours, with Justices Mathew, Grantham, Wills, and Kennedy. I went to the Guildhall Banquet tonight. Lord Salisbury was a trifle sarcastic about the 'Concert of Europe', which, he said, 'preserves peace and at the same time defers for a considerable period the solution of any problem in hand.' Mr Goschen spoke for the last time as First Lord of the Admiralty, and I thought he looked, pathetically tired and old. He was characteristically gracious in his reference to his young successor, Lord Selborne, who blushed like a maiden of seventeen.

Mr Soulsby, the Lord Mayor's private secretary, who passes on from one chief magistrate to the other, told me tonight that the pay of the City Police is to be increased. They are in future to have 27s a week.

I hear from Mr Alfred Beit, the diamond millionaire, that the story of his engagement to Mrs Adolph Ladenburg, of New York, is unfounded. The story has been going the rounds. Mrs Ladenburg's husband, the head of the great firm of Ladenburg, Thalmann, and Co., was lost overboard on a voyage from Nassau to New York some years ago. His great fortune was left to his widow, death being assumed, but I have heard that she declares she will never remarry until she is absolutely certain that he is no longer alive.

Sir George Lewis, the solicitor [grandfather of the present Sir George], said today that with the advent of Mr Ritchie at the Home Office the friends of Mrs Maybrick, who poisoned her husband, hope to secure her release from her life sentence. She has now served about ten years. Sir Matthew White Ridley was emphatic in his refusal to pardon her, although Mrs Maybrick's mother, the Baroness de Roques, bombarded him incessantly with petitions and applications. For a time she came every morning to the Home Office.

Old Charles Morton, the manager of the Palace Theatre, is authority for the statement that the best marriage agencies in London are the long bars of the St. James and the Criterion, where the Junoesque barmaids are constantly resigning to enter the matrimonial stakes. The young men home from the Colonies are the principal suitors.

November 10, 1900.

I bought a couple of aquatints of London of the period of William IV by Boys, in an old shop behind the Royal Academy, yesterday afternoon. These very fine prints are becoming rare. As I stood in the doorway talking with the proprietor, Sam Lewis, the famous moneylender, came along. His office is close by. He stopped and I asked him about the new Moneylenders Act. Was it satisfactory and workable? 'Certainly,' he said. 'There will be less fraud, now that moneylenders have to register and disclose their real names. It is no easy business, either. Moneylenders are more sinned against than sinning, but I am dead against Shylocks. No one ever accused me of being a Shylock, and I have about a million out on loan throughout the year. I never foreclose on a really honest man if I can help it.'

Everybody is talking about the arrest of a man named Bennett on the charge of murdering his wife, known as 'Mrs Hood', who was found strangled with a bootlace on Yarmouth beach some months ago. The affair looked like going down in criminal history as the Yarmouth mystery. It is remarkable to note that people of all grades of society are more interested in crime mystery – particularly the murder of a woman – than in any other topic.

I am writing this note in the train from Calais to Paris, whither I am bound on the proposed bicycle tour with Horace Fletcher, whose objective is Venice via the Riviera. I am not sure whether I shall go all the way, but certainly to Marseilles, where I may run across Oom Paul Kruger and our old friend Dr. Leyds. The steamer from Dover was crowded with passengers, and I met many people I know – Harry Marks, of the *Financial News*, Davison Dalziel, of *Dalziel's News Agency*, who is now interested in great enterprises, including motorcars; Horace Sedger, the theatrical manager, and the Chevalier Scovel, the £75 a week tenor who married Peggy Roosevelt; Geraldine Ullmar, the comic opera star; Lady de Grey going to Paris to see Bernhardt in *L'Aiglon*; Sir A. Hardinge [now Lord Hardinge of Penshurst], who has just been appointed Minister to Persia; the Marquis de Leuville, that strange pomatumed, raven-locked poet of St Martin's Lane; Francisco Tamagno, the Turin tenor who gets £100 a night and lives on garlic and sausages; Prince Victor Napoleon, with his enormous moustache; Val Prinsep, R. A., Sir Patteson Nickalls, father of the rowing family, and Maurice Grau, the operatic manager. A notable list. The Cyclists' Touring Club have given us some invaluable information and advice about hotels abroad. They have an admirable system which enables them to tell you at a glance which is a good place to stay in and which to avoid.

DECEMBER 1901

The writer of the Diary went abroad on November 10, 1900, and as his holiday activities on the Continent have no real interest, the Diary, therefore, does not resume until December, 1901.

December 1, 1901.

From his command in the Army on account of his much discussed speech on South Africa grows apace. Today, being Sunday, I went first to Hyde Park and heard an orator tell a crowd of many thousands that Sir Redvers Buller is a national hero who has been sacrificed by the mandarins of the War Office. Loud cheers. In Clapham Common there was another great demonstration which demanded Buller's reinstatement. All over the country they are making speeches. Sir Edgar Vincent, M. P. [Viscount D'Abemon], and Mr Duke, K. C., M. P. [Lord Merrivale], are telling the west country people that they must stand by their great man. Buller has retired to his home at Crediton. The soldiers all swear by him as the man who fed his army as no man ever fed troops before. As for his military qualifications – the soldiers all say that he isn't a Napoleon.

There is a great hullabaloo about the Censor's latest refusal to license Mr. G. B. Shaw's play, *Mrs Warren's Profession*, which he wrote some years ago and cannot obtain permission to produce publicly. 'Handsome Jack' Barnes, who has read it, tells me that it is 'very French,' and that if it sees the light the playgoers of a future generation will be justified in saying that the stage of today was exceedingly daring. John Hare says it is merely 'life,' and he cannot see why the Stage Society may produce it this month, while the Censor keeps the general public away.

Mr George Gray Ward, the head of the Commercial Cable Company, arrived yesterday from New York in the *Teutonic*. He came to lunch, and was not in the least alarmed about the suggestion that Marconi's invention may in time supersede ocean cables. 'We are not at all apprehensive,' he said. 'It may become useful enough for short-distance work, but we are going on laying cables." Ward began life in London as a telegraph clerk. Now he is head of the great cable company, and, I believe, a rich man; but he says there are more chances of gaining riches in London; which is something novel nowadays, for everyone is bleating about England being 'on her last legs, unable to last another ten years,' and so on.

Mrs Arthur Griffiths, who is Kate Reilly, the dressmaker of fashion, is my authority for stating that women's fashions will undergo a great change. The long bell-shaped frocks will be less voluminous, and laced boots are to go. Also evening gowns are to be heavily embellished with ostrich plumes. Evening gowns are becoming more expensive, in the neighbourhood of £15.

December 2, 1901.

I had a letter this morning from M. Baudin, Minister of Public Works in Paris. He propounds a wonderful scheme. He wants to promote submarine cross-Channel boats to do away with seasickness. His idea is to have electric cables between Calais and Dover, on which under-sea vessels carrying two hundred passengers are to be suspended like tramcars on the roads. In case of accident the boats can rise to the surface and propel themselves with their own electric power. 'Five years from now', says M. Baudin, 'there will be no cross-Channel steamers.'

Mayo Gunn, who used to be manager of the *St James's Gazette*, under Mr Steinkopf, but who is now connected with the Wills tobacco firm (the Wills are his uncles), sends me the latest broadside against the American tobacco invasion. It is issued by the new Imperial Tobacco Company, and says: 'Americans whose markets are closed by prohibitive tariffs against British goods have declared their intention of monopolising the tobacco trade in this country. It is for the British public to decide whether British Labour, Capital, and Trade are to be subordinate to the American system of Trust, Monopoly, and all that is implied therein.'

Mayo Gunn adds that the Americans will never be permitted to establish their trusts in England.

I spent last night at Finchley as the guest of Kennedy Jones in his fine new house, which was Sam Waring's special exhibit at the Paris Exhibition last year. It is filled with all sorts of wonderful improvements and inventions, including a marvellous gramophone, which is quite free from irksome scraping sounds. Finchley is only a few miles out, but it might be far in the country, with its expanse of fields and meadows. We came back this morning in K. J.'s big new auto car of fifteen horsepower. It goes uphill almost as easily as on the flat. It is a great change in K. J.'s circumstances.

I remember him eight or nine years ago, when he was a reporter on T. P. O'Connor's evening paper *The Sun*. Then he was prosperous on seven or eight pounds a week. He joined Alfred Harmsworth, and now he has an income of at least £25,000 a year.

I met young Santos Dumont, the clever Brazilian inventor of the flying machine, with Mrs Arthur Stannard (*Booties' Baby*) today. He says there must be a lot of development and much disappointment before people will be able to use flying machines – if ever, but he means to persist. He speaks English fluently, and appears to be a modest young man, quite unaffected by all the adulation that has been heaped on him, particularly by the women of France and England. He talks quite modestly of his wonderful feat in flying round the Eiffel Tower in Paris, as if it were an everyday occurrence like driving in a hansom cab.

December 3, 1901.

Sir Francis Jeune [President of the Admiralty and Divorce Division, afterwards Lord St Hilier] was ambling along in Carey Street, behind the Law Courts, as I came down there. He was in a grim humour. 'I don't know', he said, 'that I wouldn't prefer to come up in this street (where the bankrupts go for examination) than to be put through a grilling in the Divorce Court at the hands of Bargrave Deane. I have just finished a dreadful day, and the air in those rooms is overpowering. I go through a Black Hole of Calcutta experience every day. It is enough to sour a saint.' A most kindly old man, certainly one of the saintliest I know. He keeps fit by riding his bicycle. The favourite jest in the suburbs is, I hear: 'I think I shall have to tell Sir Francis about you.'

Commodity prices have not changed much. In this bitter weather I have had to order in some household coal at 19s 6d a ton. Provision markets are what they call 'steady' – Scotch salmon is 2s, soles 1s to 1s 2d, plaice 5s to 6s per stone, whitebait 1s per quart, Yorkshire fowls 2s 6d, Surrey 2s 6d to 3s, Irish 1s 6d to 1s 9d.

I went last night to see Marie Tempest in Becky Sharpe at the *Prince of Wales*. She has become the complete actress – a great change since I first saw her a dozen or more years ago in *The Red Hussar*, as a musical comedy star. She does not look a day older than she did then, and is just as vivacious.

Seymour Bell, who represents the London Chamber of Commerce in America, tells me that Americans are beginning to drink Scotch whisky, and that it will soon be a popular beverage. They call it 'High Ball', and drink it with ice and soda. He also says that unless we begin to adopt labour saving devices in England the Americans will soon beat us in manufacturing.

All the experts are beginning to agree that the omnibus, if not exactly doomed to extinction, has a dubious future. Mr Clifton Robinson, who is strong on private tramways, and Mr John Benn [Sir John] of the County Council, are firm in this belief. Mr Yerkes thinks that when the Metropolitan and District are fully electrified, the omnibuses will have a bad time. This belief is reflected, too, in the market position of the omnibus company. A year ago the London General Company's shares were 216. Today they are 100. The £6 shares of the Road Car Company stood a year ago at 10¼. Now they are 4½. The Stock Exchange, at any rate, is taking no chances.

I wonder why people do not use auto cars more for commercial purposes? Newspapers, for instance, ought to utilise them more. When I was in Paris last week I went to the office of Journal, and there they have installed twenty-five autocars for the delivery of their papers. That is an enormous number, but they seem to have made a success of it.

December 4, 1901.

Hector MacDonald has been giving me a good deal of trouble. [Major-General Sir Hector MacDonald, a famous and popular soldier who started life as a draper's assistant, committed suicide in Paris some years later.] It appears that the MacDonalds of the Empire subscribed a large sum to provide their hero with a sword of honour to commemorate his famous tactical movement at the battle of Omdurman. The sword was made by an Edinburgh goldsmith named MacDonald. The secretary of the committee which ordered the sword, also a MacDonald, told me that when the sword was delivered to Sir Hector at Capetown during the present campaign [Boer War] it was found that it was merely a cheap so-called tailor's sword, and not the bejewelled work of art that had cost so much money. We printed this – as illustrating a piece of Scotch economy – relying on the apparently unquestionable authority of the official MacDonald. But the Edinburgh jeweller, a man of integrity and good character, sued for damages. We could not prove our case. Sir Hector is off chasing De Wet with his Highland Brigade, and is unapproachable – and so we agree to pay £800 in full liquidation without going to trial.

I had a prolonged chat with an omnibus driver all the way to the City from Sloane Square. The old man must be over seventy, but looks quite young. They now have a 'Busmen's Union, and they are beginning to agitate for a day off now and then without being fined for it. They work 365 days a year, and think that too much. Besides, the pay is bad – never above £2 a week, including extras. Out of this rents have to be paid at an average of 7s 6d a week, and food, so that there is not much over for beer.

Mr Alpheus Cleophas Morton, MP, came into the office to enlist my interest against the purchase of the National Telephone Company by the Government for something like £8 million. He talked fiercely for half an hour, and at the end of that time I could not understand if he was for or against the scheme. Anyhow, I see little chance for the company, for Lord Londonderry, the P. M. G., declines to permit them to lay any more wires underground, and since they are not permitted to string them on poles, their usefulness for future development is clearly at an end. The Government will surely make a hash of the telephones if they are taken over.

A dreadful scene this afternoon in Bedford Street, near the Strand. Two drunken viragos fighting; one of them handicapped by having an infant in her arms. A couple of dozen loafers cheering them, and a policeman who stood by only interfered when one of the women showed 'claret' on the nose. No use remonstrating. The police know how to handle these people. When it was over they all adjourned to the beerhouse at the corner.

December 6, 1901.

Maude Garland, the statesque Juno who used to stir the hearts of our young Guardsmen at the Gaiety, had a bad fall in the Park this morning, and was taken into St George's Hospital severely bruised. She was ambling along the Row where there was an unexpected fusillade of shots, which sent her hired hack skeltering and displaying unwonted alacrity like a buckjumper, and she came down in a heap. It seems that 'George Ranger' (the Duke of Cambridge), who is the autocrat of the Park, has decreed that there are too many wild ducks, which are corrupting the manners of the tame ones, and so every morning he organises a battue. The result is recorded across the way at St George's, where the equestrian casualties are deposited. Someone suggested to the Duke yesterday that the ducks might more easily be snared. His reply, as usual, was vigorous.

Teixeira de Mattos, the Dutch translator, took me today to Pembroke Gardens to see Samuel Smiles, the author of *Self-Help*. I thought he had died years and years ago. He is, in fact, nearly ninety years old, and very feeble. The old gentleman is more proud of the fact that he was once secretary of the South-Eastern Railway than of his literary efforts. He told me that he began life as a medical man in Scotland, but could not make a living, so he became editor of the *Leeds Times*, and then a railwayman. He thinks

George and Robert Stephenson were extraordinary men. Also James Nasmyth; and he is sure that women in England have more freedom now than they have ever had. A kindly old gentleman, with a sense of humour.

His Majesty the King came back from his Sandringham shooting party today. I saw him in his carriage driving down Pall Mall with his customary big cigar in his lips. He had with him Herr von Pfyffer, his German secretary, which leads one to believe that His Majesty is preparing himself for a visit either to or from his much-beloved nephew, the German Kaiser. The latter always tries to speak English with his august uncle and King Edward, who for some reason or other has never taken William to his bosom invariably retaliates in German.

Further down the street I ran into General Kelly-Kenny, one of the heroes of the Boer War. He has just come home. He thinks the war is likely to last several years longer. 'It wouldn't last a month,' he said, 'if some of these politicians like Campbell-Bannerman and 'Bob' Reid [Lord Lorebum] and Lloyd George were not so indiscreet in making pro-Boer speeches.' At lunch today at the Café Royal there was John Philip Sousa, the conductor of the famous American band. He has just been playing before the King and Queen at Sandringham. He says the thing that struck him most was the simplicity of it all. He expected to see crowns and coronets and tiaras all over the place. Instead of that 'the King came in from shooting looking just like any old farmer in Kentucky. What did he like best in our programme? Well, I think he was divided between *Swanee River* and *Rule Britannia*! He's very musical.

December 7, 1901.

George Lewis, the lawyer, tells me that Whitaker Wright is to come up for public examination at the Bankruptcy

Court next month to explain the collapse of the British America Corporation, the London and Globe, and the disappearance of the immense profits made in the Le Roi No. 2 'deal'. The disappearance of a capital of £1,500,000 in one company, which now has only £157 left, will be another question to answer. Rufus Isaacs [Lord Reading] will probably cross-examine him, and if he does it will be a duel of wits, for Wright is a wizard with figures, and the great lawyer knows the Stock Exchange in and out. Meanwhile, Whitaker Wright continues to live at Lea Park, in Surrey, with its wonderful artificially made lake over the smoking-room. His town house in Park Lane, next to Lord Londonderry's house, is still open. The Marquis of Dufferin, ex-Viceroy of India, who was one of Wright's 'shop window' directors, has lost a vast sum in these City enterprises. He has, I hear, retired to Clandeboye, terribly upset at the collapse.

The new Aero Club is very active, and proposes to make ballooning a popular pastime. This morning I met the Hon. Charlie Rolls, inseparable from his auto car, on his way to the Crystal Palace, where he is to fly this afternoon. He tells me that the club proposes to organise a series of balloon flights next spring, and to offer some big prizes. Later in the day I had a call from the Rev. J. M. Bacon, the little parson aeronaut – a sky pilot in more senses than one – who lives at Newbury. He wants to do some night ascents and photograph St. Paul's dome by moonlight. 'I was stepping into the car of my balloon the other day', he said, 'when a man who evidently doesn't like me came along and stopped. He pointed at me and said to a man with him, 'Look at one gasbag about to carry another.' I turned round and nearly forgot my cloth. What I meant to say was 'You can go to hell.' I checked myself and merely glared. 'All right', he cried. 'Don't explode. Your balloon will do that for you soon enough.'

Mr Rolls told me that the Automobile Club are going to propose that they will no longer oppose the compulsory fixing of identification numbers or letters on auto cars provided that the absurd twelve mile limit is abolished and the speed limit is left open, so that people may only be prosecuted when they drive dangerously. They are much cheered by Mr Henry Chaplin's [Viscount Chaplin] public statement that in his opinion twenty-five miles per hour is not an excessive speed, and it is not dangerous provided brakes are sound and drivers are safe. The principal danger, to my mind, is still the difficulty of controlling restive horses, particularly on country roads, when swift moving auto cars approach.

Potter, the boot maker in Regent Street, near Portland Place, is dead, and I hear his business is closed. I have alternated between him and the old shop in the arcade of Her Majesty's Opera House in Pall Mall [Carlton Hotel]. Latterly I find that many people are taking to ready-made boots on the American plan. They are quite cheap, from 15s to £1 per pair, against the handmade price of £1 15s, but in the end I think the ready-made boot is dearer. Also it is not always made of real leather.

December 8, 1901.

There have been some fine medieval scenes in the House of Lords before the Court of Claims, and also some fine fees for the lawyers. Mr G. Sotheron-Estcourt claims, as owner of the manor of Shipton Moyne, to be Chief Larderer to His Majesty; the Earl of Denbigh demands his right to be present at the Coronation as Grand Carver; Sir W. Anstruther as Hereditary Grand Carver of Scotland; Lt. Colonel Lambert as the Waterer, and the Marquis of Ormonde as the Chief Butler of Ireland. Miss Wilshere desires to serve the King on Coronation Day with the first silver cup, but most of this was ruled out for the very good reason that there is to be no Coronation banquet.

There is a great fight on for the office of Hereditary Lord Great Chamberlain between the Earl of Ancaster, the Marquis of Cholmondeley, Earl Carrington, and the Duke of Atholl. But they will have to go before the House of Lords Committee of Privileges.

Lord Robert Cecil, K. C., tells me that he has been briefed to appear on behalf of Mr Scrymgeour, who is competing with Lord Lauderdale to bear the standard of Scotland. The fight goes back to 1670. The Duke of Newcastle claims to 'support the right arm of His Majesty while he is holding the sceptre', and he has won against Lord Shrewsbury.

I hear Mr Haldane, K. C. [Viscount Haldane], who is leader of the House of Lords Bar, has been briefed heavily on behalf of the Lord Chamberlain contestants.

For the second time this week I have, inadvertently, given a hansom cabman half a sovereign instead of sixpence. I have done it before; so have most people who do not carry a sovereign case and persist in mixing up all their currency in their pockets – gold, silver, and bronze. I can generally distinguish a sovereign in the dark, but the half coin is too near the sixpence in form and feel. Some day perhaps we shall have a change. Lord Rowton, who, as Monty Corry, was Disraeli's private secretary and projected the Rowton Houses, told me some time ago that he had proposed to 'Black Michael' that half-sovereigns should have a hole in them, like Chinese cash, in order to distinguish them, but Sir Michael laughed at him.

I had to go and see Lord Rothschild this morning at his office in St Swithin's Lane. Walter Long had warned me that if I wanted to succeed in my errand [it had something to do with a political meeting] I would do well to make a misstatement of fact on which he could correct me. The first thing the benevolent-looking old gentleman said was,

'What do you think of the Liberal chances for the next election?' 'Oh', I said airily, 'I think they have a very good chance of success.' I knew they hadn't a dog's chance. 'How are they going to do it?' I replied that I thought Campbell Bannerman's pro-Boer speeches had put him out of court as leader, and that either Harcourt or Asquith would succeed him and be successful. Lord Rothschild sat bolt upright. Then, calling to his brother Alfred, who sat at a little table at the end of the big room, he cried out: 'Listen to this pundit. He doesn't know what he is talking about. C. B. remains leader and he will lead them to defeat. Mark my words.' He was immensely pleased and shook me warmly by the hand – and granted my request.

December 9, 1901.

Dined on Saturday night at the Mansion House with Sir Joseph Dimsdale, the Lord Mayor and junior MP for the City. He is a great swell in the City and no end of a past grand officer of Freemasons, and as the Coronation will come in his term he reasonably expects to be more than the knight he now is. He will certainly be made a baronet and since he will have to carry the crystal sceptre of the City before His Majesty during the coronation ceremony, he will not escape the Victorian Order. [He got it, a K. C. V. O., and a baronetcy in 1902.] Last night was Sir Joseph's first free evening since he became Lord May or a month ago. He has to go to a City dinner every evening.

Lunched at Mr Henry Lucy's (Toby MP) – Mr Choate, the American Ambassador, Earl Cawdor, chairman of the Great Western Railway [afterwards First Lord of the Admiralty], Marion Crawford, the author, Sydney Whitman, the correspondent, Sir Michael Hicks Beach ('Black Michael'), the Chancellor of the Exchequer, who is selling his country place in Wiltshire to the State for £100,000, to be added to the Salisbury Plain camp; several ladies – and Sir Charles Dilke, who sat next to me and told me some interesting stories about gardening and fruit culture. He is a most versatile man and it is undoubted that if his career had not been so ruthlessly checked he would in time have reached the highest post in political life.

At Charing Cross this morning I was nearly run down by Lady Charles Beresford's brougham. She said she was off to Rome, where she has taken a flat for the winter. With her was her sister, Mrs Gerald Paget, and they were disputing as usual, about Woman's Rights. Mrs Paget is 'advanced' (under the tutelage of Sarah Grand) and Lady Charles an out-and-out Tory, who says all political women should be banished. Lady Charles is like a Frenchwoman, in that she is most generous in the use of rouge. Lord Charles, who is second in command in the Mediterranean on board the *Ramillies*, will soon be coming home. There is talk of putting him up for Parliament in Hampstead. He is anxious to come back and have another go at 'My Lords of the Admiralty'.

Arthur Collins told me that the pantomime at Drury Lane this season is going to beat the record for gorgeousness. He had devised a wonderful dragon with electric eyes and steam pipes inside, but has had to give it up because the contraption gets so hot inside that the workmen who operate it go frantic with terror and rage. At a dress rehearsal yesterday, just as a singer was in the middle of a sentimental song and the dragon upstage was twisting its eyes, the whole theatre was startled with: 'Oh – murder! 'Ow long is this d ... thing goin' on burnin' me up?' They are afraid to risk it on the first night.

December 10, 1901.

I remember going to Vienna about ten years ago to be shocked at the sight of several women smoking cigars. We appear to be progressing towards that end here. After dinner last night at the Carlton I saw four women in the lounge smoking cigarettes quite unconcernedly. One of them had a golden case, and she was what is called a chain smoker. Dr Gunton, who was with me, told me that most women now smoke at home. 'That's what makes them so nervy', he said, 'but when I tax them with over-smoking they nearly always deny it.'

In the new Kingsway street, which will one day be a splendid avenue, I bought this morning a fine Queen Anne walnut table, with drawers, all in excellent state, for £1 10s. Also a pair of exquisitely-made Queen Anne-style Sheffield plate candelabra for £2, and a mahogany knife- box for ten shillings. They were all worth much more. The dealer wanted to press on me a dozen linen-fold oak panels for £3, but though they were quite genuine, and in good condition, I declined, because I can get all I want in Essex for half the money.

'B. P.' [General Baden-Powell] is tired of the adulation which he gets wherever he goes. He says he still cannot go to a theatre or public place without being cheered at and mobbed. The hero of Mafeking is going back to Africa this month to take charge of a new force of Colonial police. There will be 20,000 men and 30,000 horses to cover a territory of 200,000 square miles in the Transvaal and Orange River Colony. The late Queen Victoria never forgave him for having sketched his own portrait on the emergency stamps that he devised for Mafeking during the siege.

The revival of *Iolanthe*, after nineteen years, has brought Mr W. S. Gilbert from his retirement at Harrow, to superintend the rehearsals. He is very sad about it all, for both Sir Arthur Sullivan and D'Oyly Carte have died in the past year or so, and he misses all the old faces. George Grossmith [father of the present G. G.] is now an entertainer, Jessie Bond, the original 'Iolanthe,' has retired; Miss Fortescue, whose fairyness in the piece inflamed the passion of a real and not a fairy peer, and won her damages for breach of promise, devotes herself to a superior art; and Rutland Barrington is singing at Daly's. Gilbert is very critical of the new lot.

I saw a large hatchment with a great coat of arms over the portico of a house in Grosvenor Square today, the first for some years, to indicate the death of the owner. This fashion of displaying mourning seems to go more and more into disuse.

December 11, 1901.

I took half an hour after dinner last night, on my way to the office, and looked in at the Royal Aquarium to watch the big ping-pong tournament. There was a crowd around the eight tables. Some of the play was shocking. I could have done better on a kitchen table. The best work was done by Roper Barrett, the tennis player, who defeated Launceston Elliott. Mr T. Jeffries was eventually declared the winner over all. The Aquarium was terribly cold and draughty in this dreadful wintry weather. Two rival ping-pong associations are now in full swing, and it threatens to become one of the national pastimes.

Commander Kelly, of the United States Navy, came to see me today, and told me about the new Holland submersible destroyer Fulton, in which he went down off Long Island and remained under water for fifteen hours. English and French boats of this description have been submerged for various hours, but none so long as this, so far the severest test. The crew slept, ate, and played cards, and on coming up said they had been in no way inconvenienced by the battle of the elements that had been raging above. Commander Kelly thinks that in ten years there will be no surface ships of war on the water.

I lunched today with Charles Frohman, and he informed me that in his opinion England would always be the supply depot for American theatres. 'You see', he said, 'our American young men will not go in for authorship because they can do better in commerce. When a young man of talent comes out of Yale or Harvard he is at once snapped up by Wall Street with a good salary, and he has no inclination to risk failure and possible penury. It is different here. I simply have to come to London for plays, and I think it will always be so.' Frohman is interested in *Bluebell in Fairyland*, which is playing at the Vaudeville with Seymour Hicks and Ellaline Terriss in the cast, and he thinks that Hicks is the most intelligent actor on the English stage today. 'Some day', he says, 'Hicks will make a hit as Hamlet.' The great little man and I talked reminiscently of the days long ago when I first met him as an advance agent for Haverley's minstrels.

Now that straw has been removed from the floors of our omnibuses, the London General Company has decided to pursue its onward march. I came down to Fleet Street tonight in an omnibus brilliantly lighted by an acetylene lamp, so strong that one could almost read with it. The conductor told me that all the cars are to be lighted with acetylene.

December 13, 1901.

A letter today from John Redmond, in New York, where he proposes to embark for home this week. Says he has been promised a goodly sum for the Irish Party, though his visit was not primarily financial. He complains that the collections are becoming attenuated owing to the fact that the Irish servant girls, who used to contribute regularly every week throughout the country, are not so much interested as they were ten years ago. Even the Irish music-hall actor, who was such a great propagandist with his sentimental songs about 'the dear old country' is becoming scarce and not so popular. 'We had a meeting the other evening at the Cooper Union Hall', writes John Redmond, 'and the audience sang "Kathleen Mavourneen." Only a few of them seemed to know the words, which shows a great change.'

Lady Londonderry does not like the photograph of her which one of the illustrated papers printed this week. She thinks a photograph should be really life like if it is to be useful, and she has sent me one (with a characteristic note) which I think will not come under such criticism. Her daughter, Lady Helen Stewart, is to marry young Lord Stavordale, heir to Lord Ilchester, next month, and it will be the wedding of the year, for she is not only a great figure among the younger women of society, but she will one day, in due course, become mistress of Holland House and its great traditions. I presume the wedding will be at St. George's, Hanover Square, since that is now the most fashionable church in town.

I bought some Christmas champagne at Berry Brothers today. The duty has gone up from 6s to 7s 6d, and prices look to me much too high even for a luxury beverage. The best Clicquot, Heidsieck, Moet Chandon, and so on are fetching about 93s. There are various less fashionable brands at about 85s, and this is a fair advance on six or seven years ago. Russia and the United States are yearly taking more and more of the French sweet champagnes, and if prices continue to rise here I shall not be surprised to see the wine go out of use altogether. Burgundies and clarets are much more popular.

Christmas trade is not very good, I am told. The majority of the stuff one sees in the shops is of cheap foreign manufacture, mostly German. People are going about saying they will not buy German goods because of the violent anti-English pro-Boer attitude of the Germans, but they buy German goods just the same. There is not much to choose between the Germans and the French in the matter of pro-Boerism. Harry Marks, of the *Financial*

News, told me yesterday that he was several times grossly insulted in the streets of Paris. '*A bas les Anglais*' and '*Rosbif*' appear to be favourite terms of endearment on the boulevards.

December 14, 1901.

Captain Nicholas, who is in charge of the royal mews at Buckingham Palace, showed me over the place. The long line of loose boxes, filled with the famous Hanoverian creams which draw the State carriages, made a most impressive spectacle. The horses are tended with great care, and are exercised daily by the small regiment of grooms who are employed at the mews all the year round. The creams trace their ancestry to the first four that were brought over from Hanover by King George I., and no other breed has been employed in State processions 'What about the automobile?' I asked Captain Nicholas. 'Not a chance', he replied. 'These creams will be employed by the Kings of England so long as there are kings.'

Max O'Rell, otherwise Paul Blouet, who is on a lecturing tour in the United States, has sent me a copy of his latest book, *Her Royal Highness Woman*, with a characteristic note, to the effect that 'it is the best book I have ever written.' He has sent me every first copy of his many books, and always with the same modest description. I have often asked him to write his experiences as a French prisoner at Sedan and of his part in the Commune fighting, but he prefers to devote himself to John Bull and his people. More money in it.

Phil May is talking of producing a weekly illustrated paper on the lines of *Punch*. He is encouraged thereto by the success of his *Annual*. He will have to be careful not to meet the fate of his colleague, Harry Furniss, who deserted *Punch* to found *Lika Joko*, and made a dismal failure. Besides, I do not think May is now physically strong enough to go through the strain of founding a weekly. Furniss told me the other day that in spite of his great success on *Punch*, George du Maurier never received more than £1,000 a year, and had to make up the rest by lecturing; which was not much. Affluence only came to du Maurier eight or nine years ago with *Trilby* and *Peter Ibbetson*. The Harpers paid him the enormous sum of £10,000 on the delivery of the MSS. of the latter indifferent story.

Had a call today from Michael Maybrick, the famous baritone, who said he had received a piteous letter from the old Baroness de Roques, Mrs Maybrick's mother, asking him to help her in her appeal for her daughter's release from prison! Mrs Maybrick, his sister-in-law [sentenced for life for the poisoning of her husband, was released in 1904], has been in Woking and St Albans prisons for sixteen years, and her mother has spent her fortune in attempting to obtain her freedom.

December 15, 1901.

Harry Cust, Schomberg McDonnell (Lord Salisbury's secretary), and I lunched at the Café Royal. We were discussing the abomination of mud splashes to which pedestrians are subjected from horses' hoofs in the streets. We finally came to a wager. Each of us was to walk a certain distance and the one who came back without a spot of mud on his collar was to have £1 from the other two. If two were free, the remaining third would have to pay each £1, and if all were free, the bet was off. We were to return at once by cab to the Café Royal and compare results. Each man was to walk close to the kerb and not try to dodge mud splashes, Cust to Hyde Park Corner and along Piccadilly, McDonnell to the Haymarket and the Strand to Wellington Street, and I to Oxford Circus.

I had not gone two hundred yards when I received a great blob of mud on my neck and collar and so did not consider it worthwhile going on, and returned. Within ten minutes Cust and McDonnell also came back, each fully decorated with mud splashes. All bets off!

My hansom cab driver who calls for me every morning at two o'clock after we have sent the paper to press informed me this morning that his brother, who is also a cabman, is taking lessons in automobile driving in the hope that some day he will be able to drive a horseless cab. I told him it would be a good idea if he, too, took lessons, but he shouted through the opening at the top that he wasn't going to waste his money on such foolishness. 'Them automobiles', he said, 'are all right as playthings, but you can't depend on 'em. Besides, they are dangerous and you can't guarantee getting your fare to the place he wants to reach. You'll never beat my old 'orse.'

I wonder if he is right. You don't always reach your destination by motor, but I do not think the hansom cab has much to brag about on the score of safety, especially on a slippery road.

Arthur Lawrence, the editor of Cecil Harmsworth's *Liberal Review*, has sent me a cheque for £10 for my article on my weekend cottage experiences in Essex; which is considered fair pay for 3,000 words. A good many amateur writers are breaking into the pages of the reviews these days, and that keeps the prices down, for these amateurs are quite pleased to see their effusions in print without emolument. *Harper's Magazine* has sent me a cheque for £20 for an article on the 100 Years' War in Achin. That is somewhat nearer the market value, but I notice that in America also there is a tendency occasionally to go outside the ranks of the professional writers. Julian Ralph, the war correspondent states that on several occasions *Harper's* have paid him as high as £100 for an article, but he has had to carry his own expenses in such cases.

December 16, 1901.

A neat little egg-box came to me today. It contained a dozen nice brown eggs, on top of which was a card: 'Compliments of the season from Dan Leno.' Few people know that this most popular of all comedians is an agriculturalist as well! He has a 'farm' of an acre or so back of his house in Clapham Park, and there he grows cabbages and potatoes, poultry, butter, eggs, and so on. He is probably the highest paid funny man in the world.

My friend X——, who took part in the march on Peking against the Boxers, has come back, and has presented me with a magnificent Japanese sword, with jewelled hilt and wonderfully fashioned scabbard. It was a present from one of the Japanese Mikados to the Son of Heaven, and X—— says he bought it for next to nothing at auction from a Russian soldier who had looted it from the palace. I have noticed for some time in Bond Street windows a varied collection of jade ornaments, silken gowns, and exquisite carvings, all of it part of the international army's loot. The rifling of the Chinese treasure house – a collection of works of art that has occupied the labours of centuries – reflects no credit on our civilisation; but I am always glad to hear that the British were not to the forefront in looting.

The big storm that has now passed was the worst for a quarter of a century. Many places have been isolated for two or three days. Never have so many telegraph lines been down, and, as for snow, the usual 'oldest inhabitant' tales are prevalent in the north. The landlines have been so disrupted that on Saturday the cables to America were held up, and there were rumours in New York that London was in the throes of a panic.

I met, today for the first time Mrs Glyn (Elinor Glyn), the much-talked-of Essex society woman who's *Visits of Elizabeth* have created so much interest in and out of

London. I saw her first at Mrs Arthur Paget's Charity Tableaux at Her Majesty's Theatre. She is a striking figure, and is full of new ideas on literature, and so full of energy that nothing will deter her from finding expression for them.

At dinner last night I met Mr F. C. Burnand, who was for so many years editor of *Punch*. He had been connected with the paper for over forty years. We talked of pantomimes that are just now in full preparation, and he says it is hard work writing them. He is joint author of this year's effort at Drury Lane. He is an inveterate punster. While at Eton he explained his unwillingness to play football because he was 'more shinned against than sinning'. Later in a conversation with Cardinal Manning he said he was inclined to the stage rather than the Church as a vocation. The Cardinal retorted: 'You might as well say that to be a cobbler is a vocation.' Burnand answered quickly: 'In that case I should still have the cure of soles.' He told me that his *Black-Eyed Susan* had a record run of 800 nights, and in his seventy years of life he has perpetrated over 100 plays.

December 17, 1901.

I have had some correspondence recently with Mr Clemens (Mark Twain), who writes to me from Hartford, in Connecticut, that he has had an interesting controversy with the great Professor Virchow, who lives in Berlin. When Mr Clemens was in London a little while ago he lived in Tedworth Square, Chelsea, where I used to go occasionally to play a game of pool with him. He was then deeply interested in an Austrian food preparation. With the late John M. Bergheim, the Galician oil engineer, he formed the Plasmon Company. Mark Twain said he was going to recover the fortune he lost in his book publishing venture. He began to bombard the scientists of Europe with letters on the subject of food values, metabolism, and so on. The Virchow correspondence went on over a period of years. Now Mark Twain writes, 'I have had a stunner from Virchow on what he calls Cellular Chirography. I have never seen so many long words. They twirl and twist like a cowboy's lariat. I have responded today by sending him a copy of my new book, *The Man that Corrupted Hadleyburg*. Let him chew on that awhile.'

The police are very active now in suppressing omnibus racing, which is becoming dangerous. I was on a Road Car omnibus today in Whitehall. A London General Company omnibus pulled up alongside. Next came a pirate. They all started at once, and the drivers lashed the horses into a gallop, the while the vehicles rocked like boats. The passengers got excited, and one man's top hat blew off. When we got to Trafalgar Square the Road Car was leading by a length, and the pirate, with his starved horses, was one hundred yards behind. The new rate of a penny from Charing Cross to the Bank seems to act as a magnet to the former point, and the rivals take great risks in getting there first.

Mr Pirrie [Lord Pirrie], of Harland and Wolff's shipbuilding yard, gave me today a pamphlet about liquid fuel for steamships. He thinks highly of it, and says that if proper supplies of oil could be arranged he sees no reason why coal bunkers should not be discarded. He told me that Sir Marcus Samuel [Lord Bearsted] and Sir Fortescue Flannery, MP, the marine engineer, have almost convinced him, but he is not yet sure what effect the proposed fuel will have on the speed of liners.

Charles Balch, the manager of the Absent-Minded Beggar Fund, which has been raised by public subscription for the benefit of the soldiers in the Boer War, has asked me to go down to Alton to inspect the new buildings, which have cost a mint of money. They have taken over £100,000. Mrs Brown Potter's nightly recitation of Kipling's *Cook's Son, Duke's Son* has been the greatest money-getter for the fund. She recited last night at the Hotel Cecil, and filled two soap boxes with sovereigns and half-sovereigns.

December 18, 1901.

Of all the hundreds of men about town whom one meets there are few more picturesque than old Captain Blyth, who talked for a few minutes in Piccadilly this afternoon. He is always immaculate. His hat is shiny, his boots are shiny, and his spirit scintillates. He told me of the good old days in the early sixties when he drove a coach from London to Reading as an amateur whip, and of the people whom he used to drive. Captain Blyth is the hero of a great story that is told of him. Once he was having his hat ironed in a hat-shop in St. James's Street. A certain Archbishop of Canterbury entered and, taking the bare-headed Captain Blyth for a shop man, handed him his shovel hat and said: 'Have you got a hat like that?'

'No, I haven't', answered Blyth, to the surprise and horror of the archbishop, 'and if I had I'm damned if I'd put the pesky thing on my head!'

Lord Rosebery has come out of his lone furrow at last and made a speech at Chesterfield, which looks like a bid for the resumption of Liberal leadership. The Liberals are terribly puzzled because it was an old-time Whig speech almost designed to drag Joseph Chamberlain and the Duke of Devonshire away from the Liberal-Unionists into a resurrected Whig organisation. But while Lord Rosebery is threatening to make six more important speeches it does not look like much more than speechifying. 'C. B.' is reported to have said that Rosebery is too rich and intellectual to be much of a danger to the Unionists, and too indeterminate to be of much use to the Liberals.

Billington, the hangman, is dead. He was something of a character, and he took great pride in his 'profession', but he had to hang Patrick McKenna at Manchester a fortnight ago, and that upset him, for McKenna was a bosom friend and townsman of his at Bolton. Billington's complaint recently was that the authorities do not seem to appreciate the importance of the hangman as they formerly did. He used to get oysters and champagne for breakfast before executions. Now this has been reduced to bacon and eggs and tea; but the fee of 10 remains. Billington always maintained that Dr. Neill Cream, the notorious woman poisoner, was 'Jack the Ripper'. On the scaffold Cream suddenly called out: 'I am Jack.' Before he could get any further Billington pulled the bolt and Cream was no more. Billington, however, was convinced that had he waited a second longer the words 'the Ripper' would have been uttered. The mutilation of the Whitechapel victims was undoubtedly done by a hand skilled in surgery, and the murders ceased after Cream's arrest.

December 20, 1901.

Everybody is discussing the affair at Birmingham where a crowd of 40,000 people surrounded the town hall and wrecked all its windows because Mr Lloyd George, MP, was trying to make a pro-Boer speech. Lloyd George was finally smuggled out. Disguised as a policeman he marched out with a file of constables, and policeman 87D, greatly daring, followed in the MP's clothes. Lloyd George fell out of the ranks at the word of command and got his clothes back later. He puts it all down to the Chamberlain party that rules Birmingham, and will not hear any side but their own. The uproar at the town hall was terrific, and the place looks like a ruined factory.

The new hotel in Piccadilly, which Mr Sherry was reported to have in contemplation on the site of Walsingham House [now the Ritz] is not to be built after all. Lord Walsingham sent down a letter tonight saying there is no truth in the report, and that Walsingham House is not to be sold.

Mr Harris, of the Carlton, says there are enough first-class hotels in London to meet all demands, but judging by the requests for rooms for next year's coronation, this does not appear to be correct.

Moberly Bell (manager of *The Times*) told me tonight – not for publication – that old de Blowitz, the famous Paris correspondent, is coming to the end of his tether. He is rather feeble now and somewhat *exigeant* as well. They have had in training a young American, named Fullerton, who, Moberly Bell thinks, will be able to take de Blowitz's place soon. To my mind the Paris correspondence of *The Times* has not been as good lately as that of the otherwise heavy *Daily News*, whose correspondent, Mrs Crawford, appears to lead a long way.

Mr. Gladstone used to say that while de Blowitz was pontifical and only occasionally newsy and Mrs Crawford entertaining and modern and represented his Liberal viewpoint he was yet far more impressed with the daily despatches of Mr. Farman of *The Standard*.

Business seems to be encroaching everywhere. Victoria Street, which is taken up entirely with residential flats, is being commercialised. Here and there the ground floors are being taken up by shops. They say that the American Legation, which has been in Victoria Street for years, is likely not to renew its lease on expiry. That, too, I suppose, will be turned into a shop some day. Somehow or other residential flats do not flourish in England as they do elsewhere. The Englishman prefers his house and his garden. Besides, flats, if they are at all good, are dearer than houses.

December 21, 1901.

A call this afternoon from Mr 'Monty' Guest, who had a considerable bundle of Court gossip. We talked about the coming Honours List, and he says there has been a good deal of nonsensical gossip about two rumoured peerages for two eminent financiers, Sir E—— and Sir T——, but there is nothing in it. I ventured the remark that if Whitaker Wright had not come a cropper he would have had a good chance for an honour of some sort, but he would not agree. The young King of Spain, whose coronation is to take place early in the year, is to have a signal honour; also the Czar, who, so they say, is so much like his cousin the Prince of Wales [King George V] that they might easily be mistaken one for the other.

The King and Queen will soon move to Buckingham Palace, and when they vacate Marlborough House the Prince and Princess of Wales will transfer to the latter place from York House.

I have seen the completed plans for the new processional road in the Mall, with a picture of the Arch through which traffic is to pass in and out of Charing Cross. It will be a great improvement, and when the Mall is widened and made presentable and Buckingham Palace is finally re-faced the road should be worth while.

Labouchere has been libelling John Kensit, the Church reformer, by saying of him in Truth that he is 'a publisher of a class of literature which, under the guise of demonstrating its sectarian rancour, obviously appeals simply to the depraved appetite of pruriency.' These long words have upset Kensit, especially as they constitute comment on a libel suit which he is bringing against another paper. He tried for an injunction today and failed. Very angry. This, too, on the top of a row in an Essex church on Sunday when John K—— denounced a too ritualistic vicar for wearing gorgeous vestments, swinging incense, elevating the Host and lighting great altar candles. The vicar was a former middleweight boxer and did not hesitate to 'brawl' in a sense more literal than that applied to the term in ecclesiastical circles; and John K—— came off second best.

He is a sincere, honest and most energetic fanatic.

I went to the Savage Club on Saturday night. Took with me Sir Evelyn Wood, who is soon to be a Field-Marshal, and is to command the great new training camp on Salisbury Plain when the war is over. We were entertained, as usual, by Mr Odell, the old actor, who seems to go on forever singing 'Harvest Home'; and Charles Collette, who was once a Guardsman, but is now a drawing-room and music-hall entertainer.

Between the acts at Daly's Theatre last night, where Ada Reeve is the new San Toy, George Edwardes outlined to me a scheme for a musical setting of Bret Harte's *Luck of Roaring Camp*, which he thinks might go well if Morton and Monckton put their hands to it in collaboration. I asked him why he does not get Bret Harte himself to lend a hand. Edwardes did not know that he has been living in England for years. He is down at Camberley, none too well, and Edwardes said he would write to him and, if necessary, go down and see him.

December 22, 1901.

Richard Croker, the Tammany 'Boss,' has returned from New York after a most crushing defeat at the polls, in which the Reformers once more take control of the city, only to lose it again in a year or two, for Tammany always bobs up again stronger than before. I saw the Boss at the Savoy this afternoon, and renewed an old acquaintance, for I knew him when he was plain 'Hickory-Faced Dick', with a place far down in the Tammany hierarchy. He says he has finished with politics, intends to give up his racing stables in England, and train solely in Ireland. He is a taciturn, rather surly, extremely domineering old man, with a natural capacity for managing men, and with not much refinement of manner. He was once a brakesman on a railway, but that is many years ago, and since he left off work he has accumulated a vast fortune.

That versatile writer Julia Frankau [mother of Gilbert Frankau], who, as 'Frank Danby', has gained an international reputation as a novelist, has sent me her latest literary effort. It is a book on prints which, I feel certain, will one day be regarded as authoritative and valuable to collectors. It is wonderfully illustrated with eighteenth century colour prints; a fine series of essays on stipple engravings and their work in colour. Mrs Frankau, with her talented sister, Mrs Aria and their brilliant brother 'Jimmy' Davis, the librettist of so many Gaiety successes, represents a remarkable family.

Madame Patti sang at the Albert Hall last night. I did not go, but saw her later at her hotel. It was one of her now familiar 'farewell' appearances, and she laughed gaily when I reminded her of a conversation at her castle, Craig-y-nos, in Wales, ten years ago, when she vowed that she had made her irrevocably final, farewell appearance. Patti said last night: 'I had to sing "Home, Sweet Home", of course, at the end. They never let me off without it – and do you know I forgot the words! I got to "Midst pleasures and palaces", and could not for the world think of the line, so I just mumbled it.' She was full of praise of a young pianist called William Backhaus, who played last night.

I have just seen the drawings of the new postage stamp to take the place of those bearing the likeness of Queen Victoria. The portrait of King Edward is excellent, and the design classical and pleasing. The penny stamp is to be red and the halfpenny green. Mr Henniker-Heaton, MP, the postal reformer, is agitating for the penny stamp to be made general, particularly to the Colonies and to the United States. Twopence halfpenny is too much, and blocks communication overseas.

Every omnibus today has been sporting the Rothschild blue and gold racing colours in celebration of Mr Leopold Rothschild's annual gift of a brace of pheasants for each driver and conductor. One driver had a set of yard-long ribbons on his whip, as well as rosettes on the bridles. Between four and five thousand birds were despatched from Gunnersbury Park for this occasion.

December 23, 1901.

I never knew until today that the father of Mrs Craigie (John Oliver Hobbes), the famous writer, is Mr John Morgan Richards, the leading man of the American colony in England. Mr Richards has an elaborate office at Holbom Viaduct, where he is the head of a great pill distributing business, which spends large sums in advertising every year. He has been in England over a quarter of a century without losing his American accent. England, next to America, is the greatest pill swallower in the world, and that, I learn, is the result of the Education Act of the seventies, by which the whole population became enabled to read advertisements.

I looked in at Bow Street, where Goudie, the bank clerk, with 'Dick' Burge, the pugilist, and a couple of racing men, are up for the Liverpool bank frauds, which have created such a sensation. A great battery of legal guns already on the case, led by 'Charlie' Gill, for the Crown. Goudie is defended by his fellow townsman, young Mr Smith [Lord Birkenhead], who, I am told, recently distinguished himself in the Guinea Gold litigation. Mr Smith had an enviable university career, and I judge from his manner that he has not forgotten it. He is a handsome, tall, athletic looking young man. I did not hear him speak, but I am told he has a most attractive voice and a most picturesque vocabulary. We hear, of course, the usual prophecies about him – Prime Minister, Lord Chancellor, and so on; the thing that is always said about promising youngsters. But young Mr Smith is not even in Parliament yet, and he has no family connections to push him on.

The King, in his capacity of leading the fashion, has given an order for a new all British automobile of nearly double the horse-power of his present carriage, in which he has travelled more than once between Marlborough House and Windsor as fast as it is done by train. The new carriage, which is to be made by Daimler, is to hold six people, with room beside the driver for a footman. It is to be of the double phaeton type, and will cost somewhere in the neighbourhood of £1,000.

Another of Queen Victoria's regulations is to go by the board. Drawing rooms are to be turned into Courts, which are to be held at Buckingham Palace in the evening in future, and presentations will take place there in the old manner. The number and dates of these new Courts has not yet been fixed.

December 24, 1901.

Mr James Gordon Bennett, the proprietor of *The New York Herald*, writes to me from the Villa Namouna at Beaulieu that he has sent Sidney Whitman, the correspondent, to Germany, to write a series of articles about Germany's aspirations as a world dominator. 'I have picked out Whitman', he writes, 'because he is familiar, from personal contact, with Bismarck's policy, which was imperialistic for Continental purposes; but this young man now on the throne has gone beyond that. His idea is to conquer the world and make us all his vassals. I don't like it, and I am going to stop him.' Mr. Bennett is himself an autocrat, as I know from my own experience, and he cannot contemplate another in competition, even though he is an anointed emperor.

Women are not to have the monopoly of corsets in future. In order to enjoy the proper fit of a frock coat a man should have a snug waist, and so the tailors are making propaganda for the coming era of corsets for men. My tailor sent down a sample for me to inspect today, but I did not view the thing with enthusiasm; nor do I think that most men of common sense beyond the Johnnies of Piccadilly and Bond Street will have anything to do with them.

Something ought to be done by the authorities to wipe out the scandal of the homeless people who are forced to sleep out on these wintry nights. I walked home along the Embankment this morning at two o'clock with Byron Curtis, editor of *The Standard*. Every bench from Blackfriars to Westminster Bridge was filled with shivering people, all huddled up – men, women, and children. The Salvation Army people were out giving away hot broth, but even this was merely a temporary palliative against the bitter night. At Charing Cross we encountered a man with his wife and two tiny children. They had come to town from Reading to look for work. The man had lost his few shillings, and they were stranded. We took them to Charing Cross Station, got them a hot meal, and beds for the night. This unemployment question is really a great problem. I talked with Mr Chamberlain about it the other day, and he repeated his known sentiments about our Free Trade policy being to blame for loss of work. If foreign goods were taxed the British workman would have a chance.

This being the day before Christmas has brought out everybody for final shopping, I went in a hansom along Regent Street and down Tottenham Court Road, where most of the shoppers congregate. Maple's and Shoolbred's great establishments were packed with people, and all the furniture shops in Tottenham Court Road were thronged. I notice this year a reversion to mahogany rather than the machine carved (made in Holland) black oak, with ornate sideboards. The mahogany furniture must be in the Chippendale style, which is now so popular. The black oak is disappearing into the woodsheds, for its quality has not been equal to the strain of half a dozen years. Bond Street, on the way back, was less crowded. Luxury buying is less apparent this year. Everybody is buying gramophones and ping-pong sets.

December 28, 1901.

I hear through Dr Jim [Sir Starr Jameson] that Cecil Rhodes has bought Dalham Hall, near Newmarket, which he proposes to make his permanent English home. Rhodes has never seen the place. He had a look at some photographs, which he liked, and a glance at the game book, which showed that they shot nearly 1,700 partridges in the first four days of this season, and so he characteristically instructed his agents to purchase the place. Whether he will ever go there to live is another matter. Dr Jim thinks he is much too restless to do that.

An American businessman who came to London a few days before Christmas to do a rapid deal came in to see me today to tell me his story of woe. He has been unable to do business for a week because Christmas intervened. 'This long break in England', he said, 'will one day be the undoing of this country. Wherever I go I find the doors locked. Why not have your Christmas and be done with it? Why make it a prolonged loaf? If your trade gets badly hurt one day you may put the damage down to this foolish Christmas lay-off.' He vowed that if this goes on England will be off the map in twenty years.

A New Year's present came to me today in the form of an exquisitely painted water-colour sketch with a charming note from the painter, who is none other than our old friend Joe Lyons, better known to the world as a dispenser of tea and buns. The demands of a great business career have interfered with a promising artistic career, for it is certain that if Joe Lyons had not met Mr Montague Gluckstein he would either have become a famous painter or writer, for he paints and writes with equal facility, as is illustrated by his plays written in conjunction with Cecil Raleigh and his generally praised pictures at various exhibitions. There must be at least fifty Lyons tea shops in London today, which is remarkable, for ten years ago there were few bright and attractive places where one could go for light refreshment.

When the Baroness de Bazus called today, and put on her card 'Just for a chat', I did not recognise her as Mrs Frank Leslie, the widow of the originator of American illustrated journalism. She still owns *Leslie's Weekly*, which made a great fortune in the Civil War, and left her a competency after her husband's death fifteen years ago. She has now reverted to her father's ancestral title of Baron de Bazus, conferred by St Louis. Madame remained an hour, and talked on every world subject. Also she stated emphatically that she never intended to marry the Marquis de Leuville, the minor poet of London's first nights, whose glossy curls were so much in evidence up to a few years ago. Someone says that 'de Leuville' was only a poetic fancy; that his real name was Brown or Tompkins, and that he once painted eyes for a living at Madame Tussaud's Waxworks. But that's scandal!

December 29, 1901.

A long dissertation today on 'Indeterminable Equations' propounded by my old friend Lo Feng-Luh, who was for so long private secretary to Li Hung-Chang, and is now Chinese Minister in London. Lo is the most erudite, the most persistent, and the most exacting arguer I have ever met. He is a scholar to his fingertips, and sometimes fails to hide his irritation with us ignorant Western barbarians. He told me today that when he travelled with Li Hung-Chang they spent every spare minute in philosophical argument. The old man thought Western 'civilisation' was interesting and amusing, but he was sure it could never last because of the lack of thought. 'Making wheels go round', he used to say, 'is diverting, but it does not improve the mind.' Lo told me that he is soon to go to Russia as Minister, but he prefers Portland Place to the Nevsky Prospekt.

The story that the Marquis of Salisbury is to be made a duke in this New Year's Honours List is so persistent and vouched for by so many people who ought to know, that I am almost giving it credence. I am quite sure, however, that Lord Salisbury himself is quite indifferent, and if the honour is to be conferred it must be because the King is desirous of showing that he appreciates his great gifts in spite of the considerable opposition which the Prime Minister has offered from time to time to royal suggestions. Lord Salisbury is recovering from his recent illness, and is likely to make an important speech when the House meets in a couple of weeks. He is preparing it now. Anyone who believes that all his fine speeches are impromptu makes a mistake. He is most meticulous in preparation. His speeches are often drafted beforehand and the impromptus are not omitted. One afternoon when he was entering the House of Lords he inadvertently dropped his notes. A friend picked them up a few minutes later, and glancing at them found that they began thus, 'My lords, when I entered this House this afternoon, nothing was further from my thoughts than to address your lordships.'

The fire brigade came dashing down the Strand at Wellington Street today with the usual wild cries of 'Hi! yi! hi! yi!' which always creates a sensation in the streets. One of the engine horses came down on the slippery pavement, but the men had the team going in an incredibly short time. The suggestion so often made that the firemen should abandon their wild and alarming cries and substitute a gong is bitterly opposed by the firemen. They have always yelled 'Hi! yi!' and they always will do so.

Watts Dunton, the 'shadow' of Algernon Swinburne, came along with a new essay which he thinks should stir the world. I could not make out whether he or Swinburne wrote it, and possibly it is a piece of joint authorship; something akin to a companion piece of *Rosamund Queen of the Lombards*. They hold a sort of weekly Poet's Court down at 'The Pines' in Putney, with Swinburne on a dais usually surrounded by a lot of admiring dames of the Swinburne cult, draped in Liberty clothes and all in rapture-like attention while the great man pours forth words of Putney wisdom.

December 30, 1901.

Romano, of the restaurant, in discussing with me the menus of French, Italian, and English restaurants, said that personally he preferred an English chop to the best culinary creation imaginable. He was reluctant in admitting the genius of Joseph, the great French chef, who died yesterday in Paris. Joseph was born in Birmingham, and he knew his way equally with beef and ortolans. But in order to maintain his position he had to be *Monsieur* Joseph. If he had been plain Mr. Joseph, Romano, for one, is sure that Mr Vanderbilt would not have taken him to New York to act as his chef for the unheard-of salary of £2,000 a year. Romano was bemoaning the decline of the picturesque clientele which this establishment used to boast. No more Duke of Manchester, the famous 'Kim'; gone is the Marquis of Ailesbury, who dressed and talked like a coster; ditto the sprightly 'Dolly' Tester, of the halls, and only the memory of the large sums spent on festival occasions recalls the golden days and nights of Mr. Abington Baird, the millionaire who had so much money that his purse seemed to be inexhaustible. Only the Knights of the Round Table who write the *Pink Un* seem to be left over from that remarkable gathering of eight or ten years ago.

I have been asked by Mr. Martin Knockolds, of Saffron Walden, to go down to Newmarket next Saturday to shoot hares, and I have been impelled to decline. I went last year, and it was too much for me. There must have been thirty guns, mostly neighbouring farmers, and literally hundreds of hares were driven down the wide fields and shot. I have never seen anything like it in the form of wholesale slaughter, and do not want to again. It takes a large number of beaters to do the work, and as they cost 2*s* 6*d* a day the expense of such a shoot is considerable.

Someone tells me that Mr Ritchie, who is still Home Secretary, and does not like it, is likely to be 'translated' to the Upper House. For a business man who has never been a real politician he seems to have done quite well for himself, since all the best posts are generally reserved for men of family.

The Turkish Ambassador has had his State carriage redecorated. It is a most gorgeous affair, all yellow and gold and shining metal, almost equal in splendour to the State coach in which the Austrian Ambassador takes the air on ceremonial occasions. I saw the carriage come out of Bryanston Square, where the Embassy is housed, and it was a most striking affair, to which the Pasha inside added picturesque effect. The Ambassadors are beginning to vie with the great duchesses in their State turnouts.

December 31, 1901.

The wise men of the War Office have decided that the whole Army is to be decorated with the ridiculous Brodrick cap, in which the Guards have been made to look so silly for the past year. Lord Roberts is said to be responsible. Mr Brodrick [Earl of Midleton, then War Secretary] repudiates all responsibility, although the country has fastened him with the name. It is certain that the Brodrick cap has retarded recruiting just as it is sure that whenever the red coat is discarded for something less showy the recruits will hold back. A Guards officer told me the other day that the unpopularity of the Brodrick may be gauged by the drop in the rate which nursemaids have hitherto paid the well-turned-out privates for an afternoon's walking-out. The pill box and the monkey jacket of the Household Cavalry still fetch half a crown an afternoon with beer, but the Foot Guards' Brodrick marks a distinct bear movement down to is 6d a day.

It is not often that one sees three British field-marshals walking side by side. Just outside Marlborough House today I met the Duke of Cambridge, Lord Roberts, and Prince Edward of Saxe-Weimar. Prince Edward looks rather aged now, but he is still active, and has lately been doing much entertaining at his house in Portland Place. They say he has been a most efficient soldier, but that does not mitigate his guilt in being the first man to breed the Dachshund in England.

Rider Haggard dined with me tonight, and we discussed the affairs of the world during the past year. He is, of course, full of his 'Back to the Land' ideas, and visualises England in the next generation as a happy, contented nation of small agriculturists on the Danish system. He is full of hopes on this subject. All he wants is a concerted governmental onward movement, which, he fears, is retarded by the great landed interests. For the rest we talked of the year which will be dead in a few hours as having made great history. Queen Victoria's death alone will ever mark 1901 in the story of the nation. With her departed, perhaps, the most glorious era of English history. The end of the Boer War, which was so confidently assumed with the fall of Pretoria, is not yet, and De Wet keeps a great army always on the alert. Lord Kitchener does not expect it to be over for many months. Trade has been only fair. We are on the eve of great electrification movements. The automobile has come to stay, and there are even some people who predict that in another generation our traffic will be horseless, and that the horse will disappear like the great auk. Women are coming more and more in competition with men in business, and even well-to-do girls are devoting themselves to callings other than nursing. As I write the crowds are passing down Fleet Street towards St Paul's for the usual Hogmanay jubilation at midnight. There are hundreds of Scotsmen on Ludgate Hill, all singing *Auld Lang Syne* in various dialects that suggest any place between Wick and Walthamstow.

1902

Saturday, January 18, 1902.

I came down by train from Harrow this morning with Sir Ernest Cassel, who has a house at Stanmore. He is enormously rich, and was, I believe, the son of a Frankfort banker, and he made a great fortune in Egypt. He is a British subject now, very taciturn, but kindly, though he appears to be stern. From some remarks he made I became convinced that he was the anonymous donor of the £200,000 gift to the King, which His Majesty determines to devote to the building of sanatoria for consumptive patients. The anonymity was rather puzzling to the newspapers when it was announced, and I think it was only by accident that I found it out. I taxed Sir Ernest with it, and his denial was most blundering, and not at all assuring. He has a great idea to establish a vast clinic for the study of tuberculosis. He spoke of it as if he had a vision, and his face lighted up in the most wonderful way. He is also greatly interested in the discovery of a cure for cancer, and as he is fabulously rich he will probably very soon be handing over money for this purpose.

Sir Ernest told me that he had just received word that Cecil Rhodes is ill in South Africa, and that he is not likely to live. Rhodes has chosen a place in the hills, somewhere in Rhodesia, where he intends to be buried. Dr 'Jim' told me some time ago of this curious whim.

Cassel also showed me a letter from Lord Kitchener, in which he stated that the Boers are now beginning to surrender, and are giving up arms willingly and asking for peace. It looks now as if the war in South Africa is at last actually over.

Tuesday, June 24, 1902.

I was brought out of bed early this morning, and informed that King Edward was dying after an operation. I went straight to Buckingham Palace, and there met Arthur Pearson and Alfred Harmsworth, who were there ahead of me, waiting for information, having been bidden to the Palace for this purpose. The general public at that moment knew nothing of it. It appears that the King became suddenly ill last night, and Lord Lister, Sir Francis Laking, Sir Thomas Smith, Sir Thomas Barlow, and Sir Frederick Treves were called in. Sir Frederick Treves performed the operation for what they call perityphilitis. I have never heard of it. Harmsworth says it is just plain appendicitis. This means that the coronation festivities will have to be postponed. There is consternation everywhere, as His Majesty is not out of danger.

I am told that one man in St Paul's Churchyard, who had let out a grand stand for the public to see the coronation procession, has lost £20,000.

1903

Tuesday, June 23, 1903.

Arthur Pearson aroused me from heavy slumber at 11.30 this morning. (I had been at the *Daily Express* office until 2.30) He was greatly agitated; had just come from Joseph Chamberlain, the Colonial Secretary, who had sent for him to discuss his new Tariff Reform proposals. Pearson did not, of course, know that Mr H. W. Wilson, of the Daily Mail, with his brother, Mr J. B. Wilson, of the *Daily Express*, and myself had manoeuvred this interview between the Colonial Secretary and the hesitant newspaper proprietor. The interview was arranged through another Wilson, who was Joe's secretary.

Mr Chamberlain has not until now been able to secure the support of a single London daily, and we, who are ardent Tariff Reformers, felt that it was time to see to the support of his plans, particularly since Alfred Harmsworth thunders away about 'stomach taxes'. We knew that if Joe once succeeded in talking to Pearson we would win. Pearson said to me, 'Get up. We are going to do big things. You chaps have had your way, and I have promised Mr. Chamberlain the support of the *Daily Express*.'

So I got up, and after hurried preparations for the day went to the *Daily Express* offices to help in the preparation of a pronouncement to the effect that the paper would in future advocate Mr Chamberlain's policy.

Later I went to the Colonial Office and saw Mr Chamberlain, who told me that he had arranged to have a meeting of Unionist members of Parliament. The leaders of this meeting are Mr Edward Goulding (now Lord Wargrave), Sir Alexander Henderson (now Lord Faringdon), Arthur Griffiths Boscawen (now Sir Arthur), Mr H. E. Duke (now Lord Merivale), Mr Arthur Lee (now Lord Lee of Fareham), and the Hon. M. White Ridley (late Viscount Ridley). Sir Herbert Maxwell is to be in the chair.

I am convinced that we are entering on a hectic era of political controversy, but I think that very soon now, owing to the state of the country, Tariff Reform must prevail.

After all this excitement, I decided it would be opportune to take an evening off and get some mental recreation, so I went to see Ellen Terry in *Much Ado About Nothing* at the Imperial Theatre in Westminster. She is beginning to forget her lines, but glosses it over with great charm by talking to the audience about it, and they sympathise with her. Then she goes on, having caught up the gap.

1904

Wednesday, March 24, 1904.

Spent an hour in the House of Commons to hear speaker after speaker expend energy on denunciation of the plan to carry London County Council trams across Westminster Bridge and along the Embankment. There has for some time been a determined policy on the part of the London County Council to push its public owned tram system in every direction in spite of the fact that, firstly, trams are immobile and therefore obstructive. More so now, since it is becoming increasingly apparent that swift-moving motor traffic must be the transportation method of the future. Secondly, corporation owned trams like most other publicly owned properties do not pay. But the main opposition to the scheme was the threat to ruin the Embankment by laying down rails and making half of the road useless for general traffic. The opposition in the House of Commons was of such a nature that it now seems improbable that the trams from Blackfriars Road will ever be able to go across Westminster Bridge via the Embankment. I had a good look at King Edward yesterday when he drove up to open the new wing of the Law Society's building in Chancery Lane. He was in morning dress; wore a black overcoat and black gloves. I thought he looked old and tired; and there is not much to wonder at in that, for he has been kept on the go every day for weeks. Royalty does not lay itself open to the charge of laissez faire. I take it the black gloves were worn in mourning for the old Duke of Cambridge, who was buried yesterday.

Thursday, November 3, 1904.

Arthur Pearson came into my room this afternoon and said that he had purchased *The Standard* and *Evening Standard* from the Johnstone family for £700,000. Pearson is heavily backed by men of wealth. *The Standard*, which up to three years ago, was one of the most prosperous papers in the world, has lost readers and support owing to its policy of Free Trade. I went with Pearson over the establishment in Shoe Lane tonight and found it archaic and ill-equipped for the production of a first-class newspaper. There are men there who have drawn salaries for years without doing an adequate day's work.

1905

Tuesday, July 4, 1905.

I went to the Independence Day banquet of the American Society to hear the new U. S. Ambassador make his maiden speech in London. Mr Whitelaw Reid will have to do a great deal of practising if he desires ever to match his predecessor, Mr J. H. Choate, who has just returned to America. I thought his speech exceedingly dull, which is strange, because Mr Reid as editor of *The New York Tribune* was never dull and never appeared to want for the right word. But editors are, as a rule, indifferent speakers. I did not think such a lot either of Lord Lansdowne's speech. The Foreign Secretary was in a happy enough mood, but he is one of those cold-blooded, never-warming statesmen whose precise pronunciation, even in a humorous strain, gives out the suggestion of melancholy. After dinner I talked with Lord Lansdowne about the report that Mr Reid had taken Lansdowne House in Berkeley Square for his London residence, but his lordship denied that. He said he had heard that the Ambassador was taking Dorchester House in Park Lane, the place where the Shah's son lived so gloriously about ten years ago. The house has not been permanently occupied for years since Captain Holford's father died. As for Lansdowne House, Lord Lansdowne said he could not understand how such a rumour got about. 'Of course,' he added, 'I shall never let the house outside our family. We require it ourselves.'

On my way home I stepped into the United Services Club (the senior) in Pall Mall, to see Frank Wright, and at that late hour ran into Lord Roberts, who had been lecturing somewhere tonight to officers on Imperial Defence. The old hero is all alive with his subject. 'We have learned nothing from the Boer War' he said. 'Mark my word, if we do not prepare properly for war we shall be crushed at any moment.'

It was fairly late after leaving the club, so I walked across the street and went up to see Beerbohm Tree in the 'tower' of his theatre. He was having supper with a small party. General Brabazon, whose evening clothes are the most splendid in existence, Claude Lowther, who outshines the sartorial general, and 'Sandy' Dingwall, of New York. Tree says that the theatre will go under if the Kinematograph plays are improved, as they threaten to be.

1906

Tuesday, October 23, 1906.

Witnessed a strange scene in the House of Commons this afternoon. About four o'clock there was a rush of women into the outer lobby. They attempted to hold a meeting, and for more than a quarter of an hour there was a desperate fight between the police and the women, who were led by little Mrs Pankhurst, Miss Annie Kenney, and Miss Billington. These are the same women who created a scene some months ago.

Eventually they were cleared from the House of Commons, after reinforcements of police had been brought up. There was a good deal of rough treatment and considerable horseplay, but the frail women could not resist the stronger policemen. Nevertheless, a good many police were scratched and torn.

Ten of the viragos were taken to the police station, and were charged with rioting in the House of Commons. I suppose today they will be taken to prison, where they will, of course, threaten to go on hunger strike.

Why they should go on in this fashion remains a mystery, because they know that the House of Commons will not give women votes if it can help it.

Mr Burns, of the Cunard Line, showed me today some photographs of the decorations in the new liner *Lusitania*, which was recently launched. She is the largest ship afloat, and it will take the Germans many years to overtake her. The luxury in this ship is indescribable. Suites of rooms as munificent as they are in first-class hotels. She will carry a crew of a thousand men.

1907

Monday, January 14, 1907.

Just home from the Hotel Cecil where there was a banquet to W. S. Gilbert, the librettist, to celebrate the revival of Gilbert and Sullivan operas at the Savoy. Gilbert made a speech which was quite felicitous, and he was generous to his partner, Sullivan, in saying that but for Sullivan his own name would by now have been forgotten. I sat next to Charles Santley, whose jubilee as a singer is to be celebrated in a month or so at the Albert Hall. From what I hear he is to be knighted on that occasion. To listen to Gilbert no one would ever suspect him to be the possessor of a wit that is irresistible. He looks, talks, and acts like a dyspeptic, which I believe he is. Anyhow, people who come in contact with him on short acquaintance, say he is exceedingly irascible. I cannot maintain that myself, for on two or three occasions when I have met him he has been quite affable and not in the least add.

I bought enough cloth today from W. Bill, in Great Portland Street, to fit me out for years, and shall now have to extend the experiment by finding a tailor to turn the stuff into clothes. I purchased ten yards of Irish frieze at 3s a yard. It will make a good suit and an ulster. Also six yards of 'Saxony' tweeds at 8s a yard, very solid, and half a dozen Irish hand-knitted socks at is 6d a pair, and some shooting stockings at 3s 9d per pair; which I consider considerably cheaper than in most places.

I talked with Mr E. H. Holden, MP, this afternoon. He is Managing Director of the London City and Midland Bank down in Thread needle Street. He made my head swim with figures. Their capital is over £3 million, their reserve fund likewise, and the deposits are £51 million. They have 450 branches. 'Of course', said Mr Holden, 'that is nothing compared to some of the other banks, such as the National Provincial, which has a paid-up capital of £15 million, and the Metropolitan, which has £7,500,000, or Parr's Bank with £8 million.' Then he surprised me by saying that the Union of London and Smith's Bank has £22 million subscribed capital.

1908

February 1, 1908.

The great sensation of the day is the dismissal of Sir Arthur Vicars from the post of Ulster King of Arms. The Commission of Inquiry into the theft of the jewels of the Order of St Patrick from Dublin Castle last July charge Sir Arthur with want of proper care in the custody of the strong room keys. There will, of course, be a dead set against poor Mr Birrell, the Secretary for Ireland. He is beset on all sides. Captain Craig [now Lord Craigavon], who is an Ulster MP, tells me tonight that he will ask Mr Birrell in the House on Tuesday in whose keeping the jewels were during the time they were mislaid. There is something most mysterious about the loss of these jewels, and, of course, the circumstantial rumours about highly placed people that have been going about are as thrilling as any incident in a shilling shocker. I think this Crown Jewel mystery will go down in history as a romance of the Edwardian era.

I called on the 'Pink-Un' in the Unionist Chief Whip's office [Sir Alexander Acland-Hood, afterwards Lord St Audries]. He was very red in the face, redder than usual, because of the charges of corruption among Worcester electors which have unseated Mr George Henry Williamson. 'The Pink-Un' was vehement in his remarks, and said that only a few voters had been guilty of corruption and the innocent electors were suffering disfranchisement through them. 'We are becoming a nation of priggish noodles', said the irate colonel. 'If a candidate or his agent just smile on a baby nowadays he is looked upon as a criminal. Give me the good old days of a hundred years ago.'

I hear there has been a fearful row among the young women of Swan and Edgar's staff because the firm had decided on abolishing the living-in system, and that in future their women employees should live at home or in lodgings. There has been something like a strike against this newfangled innovation.

Mrs Pankhurst's violent suffragists continue to make themselves objectionable. The four women who invaded Mr Asquith's premises in Cavendish Square with the double object of 'securing a vote and punishing base ingratitude,' were sentenced to prison yesterday by Mr Plowden. Another lot of three were sent up for six weeks by Mr Curtis Bennett [father of Sir Henry Curtis Bennett]. It is generally believed that Mrs Pankhurst's objectionable tactics will lead to

21 October 1908. Emmeline Pankhurst, Christabel Pankhurst and Flora Drummond went on trial at Bow Street Magistrates Court. (Photograph courtesy of Leonard Bentley, Flickr)

nothing, and that the women will never get the vote by such methods.

Sir John Fisher, the admiral [the late Lord Fisher of Kilverstone], asked me to lunch today to meet Admiral von Eiserdecker, Vice-Admiral von Muller, and Rear-Admiral von Giilich, of the Imperial German Navy. In a covering note Sir John said: 'Come and meet these chaps and see the sort of men we'll have to whip some day.' And then, characteristically, he added, 'Burn this.'

February 2, 1908.

I met Rudyard Kipling with his cousin, Stanley Baldwin, the young ironmaster from the West Country, who hopes one day to get into Parliament like his father before him. He stood for Kidderminster a couple of years ago as a Unionist against Banard, the sitting member. He is rather shy and not at all politician-like in his manner, and I do not suppose he will ever do more than follow his leaders if he ever gets in. But I should call him a pleasant, cultured, conscientious, but badly dressed man, without much desire to sit in the limelight; also, he has a sense of humour, and when he smiles it lights up a face that is rugged and interesting.

Lord Claud Hamilton, the chairman of the Great Eastern Railway, whom I met in the Park today, is most pessimistic about the future of the railways in this country. He attributes much of the falling off of revenue to the growing competition of tramways and motor vehicles. The suburban traffic of his line, for instance, has dropped by £36,000 and the passenger reduction by over 4 million. The time will come, he thinks, when most people will go to and from their work by motors or trams, though I cannot see how this can be done in view of the narrow and congested roads, which were not built for motor traffic. Judging by the constant motor breakdowns I should say that Lord Claud is unduly pessimistic.

A few yards on I met Fred Kottman, an old friend, who has become a successful house agent. He was once a bareback rider in a circus, and afterwards painted the waxworks at Madame Tussaud's. At one time, too, he was associated with the so-called Marquis de Leuville, with whom he shared the reputation of being able to write love lyrics with great rapidity, usually on his shirt cuffs. Kottman say he has just disposed of a number of houses in Bow, lease thirty-five years, price £275, with ground rent half a crown per annum. Several in Putney with eighty years to run, in what he calls 'a select neighbourhood', price £315 and ground rent of £6. He does not think that flats will ever replace houses, particularly now, when communication is becoming so much more efficient.

The new meter for sixpenny hansoms has come into use. I am informed that several hundred hansoms have been fitted with them. I took one at Hyde Park Corner and drove to Charing Cross. Gave the driver a penny for his tip, and to my surprise he said, 'Thank you, sir!' the usual formula, as we all know it, being, 'Can you spare it, sir?' I imagine the sixpenny cab, which has already been nicknamed 'tannercab,' will be a great success, and that the horse vehicle may now be assured a permanency.

February 4, 1908.

The assassination of the King and Crown Prince of Portugal on Saturday has created a great sensation here. The Court goes into a month's mourning, and the first Court of the season has been postponed. King Carlos was a favourite in London. I have often seen him walking unattended in Bond Street and Piccadilly. He firmly refused the attentions of Scotland Yard, always believing himself to be as safe in

London as any ordinary person. The Portuguese charge d'affaires here says that Senhor Franco, the Dictator-Premier, with the young King Manuel and the Queen Mother would succeed in squashing any republican tendencies that might be manifested. Later in the afternoon I saw Sir Henry Campbell-Bannerman, the Prime Minister, and Lord Tweedmouth on their way to Buckingham Palace, where the King received them. The Prince of Wales [now King George V] joined them there.

The slump in water colours is shown by the prices which collectors are now paying. There was a sale today at Christie's and a number of the late Edwin Long's famous works went at ridiculous prices. Fifteen pictures fetched £1,001. Twenty-five years ago one of them, *The Babylonian Marriage Market*, was sold for 6,300 guineas, and *The Suppliant* for 4,100 guineas. The highest price at today's sale was 420 guineas for an enormous canvas depicting the finding of Moses in the bulrushes. I predict that fifty years hence all of these first-class Victorian water-colour paintings will be fetching enormous prices.

Some months ago, in Paris, M. Gastinne-Renette, the French gun-maker, gave me a little target, which was a carton shot by King Carlos recently while in Paris. It proves him to have been equal to his great reputation as a revolver shot.

The carton here reproduced was made with a revolver by the King at a distance of twenty-seven yards. He fired twelve shots in fifteen seconds.

Lord Justice Vaughan Williams has taken to a motorcar! He has discarded his old brougham; which means a great deal for the march of progress.

I met Mrs Compton Keats today. She has made a success of a novel profession. She teaches housewives how to keep lamps sweet and clean and how to prevent lamp chimneys from smoking.

February 6, 1908.

Encountered the Marquis de Soveral ('The Blue Monkey') straight from Lisbon, charged with a personal message from the widowed Queen of Portugal to King Edward VIII. M. de Soveral was in Lisbon when the King and Crown Prince were killed last week. He says there is not the slightest chance of a successful republican upheaval, and is full of praise of young King Manuel's natural abilities. He is in deep mourning, having for once discarded his immaculate spats and white gloves.

I remember some twelve years ago meeting Mr Bernhard Baron, just after he had come to London to dispose of a cigarette-making machine of his own invention. Later he acquired an interest in the Carreras tobacconist shop which had received much publicity through J. M. Barrie's *My Lady Nicotine*. Baron has pushed this business vigorously in the past four or five years. I saw him again today after he had declared an interim dividend at the rate of 5 per cent per annum. The shares stand at about 16*s*, and Payton, of *Tobacco*, tells me they are good for a much higher figure.

Some of the County Council members are thinking of making war on the growing habit of showing electric signs at night. There are three or four on the Embankment which cry out in the night, and here and there in the Strand they disfigure the darkness; so that they will probably be prohibited, and London will be spared the freak advertisements which have made New York so amazingly hideous.

I was complaining today to Frank Munsey, the great American publisher, about the dearness of prices here as compared with ten years ago. He laughingly picked up a copy of the *Daily Express* and began to read from the small advertisements, 'A dainty hamper of fish direct from Grimsby, six pounds 2*s*; Russian furs, rich dark sable, brown, seven feet long, duchess stole, deep shaped collar, handsomely trimmed tails and large granny muff to match, satin lined, 12s 6d, enormous fatted fowls direct from farm at Attleboro', 5s a couple; gentleman must sell his beautiful drawing-room suite, 65s; beautiful and durable silk umbrellas, 2s 6d,' and so on. 'There's your refutation', said Munsey. 'England is the cheapest and the easiest and the freest country in the world.'

Mrs Langtry's theatre, the Imperial, which was built for her on the site of the old Aquarium in Westminster [now the Wesleyan Central Hall] does not seem to be wanted by anyone. It cost a great deal of money, and it was withdrawn from auction today at £85,000. I understand that 'Imperial' Perks [Sir Robert Perks, MP], who is the leader of the Wesleyans, wants the site for a great Wesleyan Cathedral, which will put in the shade Westminster Abbey across the way.

February 7, 1908.

I had lunch today at Stafford House, the Duke of Sutherland's palace in St James [now the London Museum], with the Right Hon. Henry Chaplin, MP [the late Viscount Chaplin]. The old gentleman, who has a suite of rooms in the house of his ducal brother-in-law, wanted to talk about a tax on foreign bacon, eggs, and cheese, but all during lunch he discoursed on the Cesare-witch, the Lincoln, and the Grand National, with here and there an anecdote about some splendid run with the Quom or the Pytchley. He said he was not feeling very well, completely off his appetite. As he said this he had his second helping of a heaped-up plate of roast goose, after a plentiful dish of fried sole. After the goose there was just a *soupçon* of cold tongue and ham, and then came a beautifully done souffle. Cheese, of course. Nor was it a teetotal meal. There was some

brown sherry, some exquisite Burgundy, and a few rounds
of port, with brandy to seal the perfection of the repast.
'You see', said the Squire, 'one can't eat very much in town.
I never really have an appetite until I've come in from a
day's hunting.'

In the Lobby of the House of Commons this evening
they were discussing a speech just made by Mr Bottomley,
who made the novel suggestion that all racing bets should
be taxed. Mr. Asquith warded him off by saying that the
subject involves a far-reaching question which he 'cannot
discuss within the limits of a Parliamentary answer.' The
State can hardly undertake to tax transactions which are
considered by law to be illegal.

Beerbohm Tree told me today that he experienced a
sudden loss of memory at His Majesty's last night in *The
Mystery of Edwin Drood*. He was standing in the middle of
the stage and had started a long speech. 'Instead of my own
part', he said, 'I was thinking of Locke's *Beloved Vagabond*,
which we are producing this week, and unconsciously
I began to speak a line which belonged to that play. I just
caught myself in time, and hitched on to Edwin Drood
again without appearing to have upset the meaning. That's
art, my boy.'

Melville Stone, the veteran of the Associated Press of
America, asked me today to make a note of the fact that
if wireless communication ever becomes commercially
successful, which he doubts owing to the absence of
secrecy, it will have a distinctive name such as Teleography
or Etherography. He is a great visionary. 'I can foresee the
time,' he said with glowing eyes, 'when people far apart will
carry on conversation without the use of wires; even as far
off as Paris or Brussels. Of course, that is a long way off;
but it is among the possibilities.'

I went into the just opened Waldorf Hotel in the new
Kingsway. It marks a wonderful step forward. The dining

room is 300 feet long and there is the largest palm room in the world. No doubt the Americans will flock to it this summer. This hotel is certainly up to the times, for in the palm room I saw three women calmly smoking cigarettes and drinking cocktails, without men to accompany them. Some of Mrs Pankhurst's legionaries, I presume.

February 8, 1908.

I am told that Brighton is regaining its place as the most fashionable resort in England. I met Admiral Lord Charles Beresford today after his return from Brighton, where he has been taking the air. He says the King and Queen Alexandra are going there next week. We talked about the Navy, and he was not particularly complimentary about Sir John Fisher, his old rival. Indeed, according to Lord Charles, the Navy is being reduced to scrap. 'If we ever have a war', he said, 'we'll be driven into harbour even by the Portuguese, because we are discarding all our best fighting material.' And so on.

Had a narrow escape from being knocked down in Whitehall this afternoon by Miss Meresia Nevill, the daughter of Lady Dorothy. She drives about rather swiftly in her high cart. The vehicle is rubber tyred, and so you can hardly hear it coming round corners. I think now that there is more danger from horse-drawn carriages than from motorcars.

I went last night to Harlow, in Essex, to 'dine and sleep', at the house of Field-Marshal Sir Evelyn Wood. A goodly party present. After dinner the F. M. kept me back and began to tell me some of his experiences in Ashanti, in Egypt, and in the Transvaal; when he had Paul Kruger in the hollow of his hand and was prevented from crushing the Boers by a telegram from Mr Gladstone. He is very diffuse and very deaf, but always comes back to the point. I never uttered a word. Useless, too, for he would not have heard me; so I sat silently and listened with interest to one of the most remarkable soldiers of our time. Finally Sir Evelyn looked up and cried, 'Gracious me! It is twelve o'clock. I had no idea we had been talking so long.' Then he put his hand on my shoulder and said, 'You know I like you because you are so interesting.'

After a fitful existence of two years *The Tribune*, the great hope of the Liberal Party, has suspended publication, and must now be numbered as one of the outstanding journalistic failures of our time. Mr Franklin Thomasson, MP, the young millionaire from the north, has lost £400,000 in the venture. It was quite a good paper, and it had an excellent and enthusiastic staff of young Liberals; but it was too political and too didactic to prevent the steady and disheartening drain of money week by week.

I have from Charles Garvice his secret of success in the making of a popular novel designed to cause every cook and housemaid in Europe and America to weep copiously. He says: 'First take a wicked Earl; then an innocent village maiden; next some irate parents, a background of soldiers and sailors, a family solicitor and an elopement scene; a church door; snow falling, detectives, and finally Villainy defeated and Virtue triumphant. There's a firm in New York who would take one of these novels a week if I could furnish it. But, alas! I can only do about six a year!' Garvice has the widest circulation of any storyteller in the United States, and though he is an Englishman he has only recently gained a footing here.

February 9, 1908.

First night of *A Woman of Kronstadt* at the Garrick last night. I have never known such enthusiasm; not so much for the play, but for the costumes. The women in the audience were fairly overcome. I asked Miss Gladys Unger, who sat next to me, to describe to me Miss Latimer's costume in the first act. Miss Unger was so excited over it that I could not follow her description, and so she said she would put it on paper and let me have it today. It is so mysterious to me that I put it down for future reference. Here it is: 'Gown of warm red face cloth draped in latest Princess style. Corsage bordered with elaborate trimming of heavy chenille embroidery, opening over a vest of ecru tucked net. The rucked sleeves are made of net to match. With the gown Miss Latimer wore a magnificent coat of red chiffon velvet with large sable cuffs and collar, and lined with fur. She also wore a sable toque and an enormous sable muff.'

Mostyn Piggott, who was with me at the Garrick, got into a little difficulty with the escort of a lady in front of us. She was in evening dress, but wore a large picture hat, and appeared to be disinclined to remove it; so that at first Mostyn could not see the stage. He leaned over and asked her to remove the hat, which she did only after considerable demur and some rather exaggerated exchange of compliments. The escort then took a hand, and, turning round, said, 'You are very impolite, sir!' Mostyn answered sweetly, 'You are, of course, a nice little gentleman.' The lady said, 'Shut up, 'Enry', and we had peace.

At Oddenino's, after the play, I saw Henniker-Heaton, MP, the great postal reformer, full of indignation against Mr Buxton, the Postmaster-General [Lord Buxton], who refuses point blank to consider penn postage to the United States. Henniker-Heaton is convinced that if the 2½ *d* rate were reduced our business with the United States would be largely increased.

Bonar Law, MP, the Glasgow iron merchant, who knows all about British trade and never fails to give a reminder of it to Lloyd George, the President of the Board of Trade, told me today that in his opinon we have come to an end of the great trade boom, which has brought in a good deal of prosperity in recent years. The imports, principally of raw materials, are down by 7 per cent, and the exports are down by 2 per cent. The figures are:

Imports

Jan., 1907	£60,534,846
Jan., 1908	£56,368,358
Decrease	£4,166,488

Exports

Jan., 1907	£43,863,883
Jan., 1908	£41,006,976
Decrease	£2,856,907

Bonar Law told me that he had just been up to see Joe Chamberlain at Prince's Gardens. He is still very ill, but overjoyed at the great victory of Mr Edward Goulding [Lord Wargrave] at Worcester on Friday. Joe thinks this victory is an infallible sign of the times, and that it portends a walk-over for Tariff Reform. Bonar is not so enthusiastic.

February 10, 1908.

We are becoming somewhat negligent in dress. Down in the City today, where I talked with the Hon. Claude Hay, MP, I noticed that he wore a soft collar, such as golfing men often wear, and brown boots. Also, he had no gloves. Many men, more than usual, go about the City in bowler hats nowadays, which shows the trend of the times.

On the other hand, as if to accentuate the difference, I had a call in the afternoon from Major-General Brabazon, the King's friend, who commanded at Pretoria during the late Boer War 'Bwab' was dressed to perfection, a wonderfully curved and polished top hat, a four-in-hand tie, long frock coat, with a lurid silk handkerchief protruding at least six inches from the pocket, as is his wont, and most immaculate white gloves. The gallant old general brushes his moustachios like the German Kaiser, and thinks the young men of today are 'simply tewwible' in their neglect of sartorial adornment.

Mr W. T. Stead is resting for a moment from the effects of newly-launched publications. He told me today that his dearest wish at the moment is to appear as Oliver Cromwell in the forthcoming London pageant. 'Cromwell', says Stead, 'was a man after my heart, and I would even go to the extent of shaving off my beard for the honour of personating that greatest of Englishmen.'

Went to see the Sicilian players tonight in Mafia at the Shaftesbury. All the social rage. I have never run through such a gamut of emotions. Signor Grasso and Signor Aguglia cycloned, stormed, hissed, wailed, wept, laughed, shouted, and stilettoed for two and a half hours, and the rest of the company aided and abetted with voice, hands, teeth, and feet. A whirling vortex of excitement. Everyone, audience as well as players, went home thoroughly exhausted.

Further political talk is about Mr Willett's perennial and never-succeeding Daylight Saving proposal, which is to come up again as a hardy annual this week. The agricultural MPs say that even if it is passed it will not succeed, because the farmers will not go against nature.

Lord Carrington [Marquis of Lincolnshire] has put his foot in it politically by declaring that labourers and chainmen employed on London's ordnance survey are sufficiently well paid at 18s a week. A man thus employed came into see me this afternoon to protest. He said it was not possible to make ends meet under 12s a week, considering that rooms are hard to get and rents are going up by shillings. 'And I'm not extravagant', he said, 'I assure you.'

February 11, 1908.

This is the era of young men. I was told in the House the other day that young Mr F. E. Smith, MP [Earl of Birkenhead] was soon to be made KC. I did not believe it because he has only been at the bar nine years. Yet here tonight I see that he is in the new list of KCs. Other new King's counsel are Mr John Simon, MP, Mr Hemmerde, MP, Mr Bailhache, and Mr Frank Russell, the latter a son of the late Lord Chief Justice. I have been watching the careers of the three first named. They ran neck and neck, and one wonders which of them will be Lord Chancellor first. They have all been going ahead very fast, but I am not so sure that taking silk will not prove somewhat of a stumbling block.

I shall not be able in future in the spring and summer months to go down to the Temple from Chelsea on board my beloved Thames steamers, for the County Council has today decided either to scrap the boats or to sell them to the highest bidder. Thus another bit of the picturesque life of the Thames goes overboard. The Council has lost an average of £50,000 a year on them. I think the fares were too high for popularity, and there were not enough boats. They ought to have run at five minute headway, like omnibuses.

Another little war is brewing, and the soldiers are all agog about an expedition which is to sally forth in India, under General Willcocks. They start from Rawalpindi about 7,000 strong, including the Gay Gordons and the pampered 10th Hussars; and they go out against some Afridis called Zakka Khels, who have been border raiding. Mr John Morley, at the India Office, was busy today giving orders, much against his peace-loving grain, but the soldiers say it will provide a fine test of Lord Kitchener's new Army organisation in India. Anyhow, every soldier whom I met tonight has been exerting his utmost to get a staff job in the new enterprise.

A note at the office from Charles Frohman, asking me to do something for an out-of-work author who wants to write some articles. Frohman spends a lot of time doing things like this. I have known him since he posted bills for a travelling show – Haverley's Minstrels – many years ago. He says incidentally that *Brewster's Millions*, which has had such success at Hicks' Theatre, in Shaftesbury Avenue, is to come off. 'I thought', he adds, 'that it was going to run for ever.'

February 15, 1908.

Lord Marcus Beresford came down from Wolferton this afternoon and told me all about Persimmon, the King's famous Derby winner, who met with a bad accident a few weeks ago. The horse, he said, had to be put in slings in a box specially erected for him. Lord Marcus, who is the King's racing manager, says he does not think any human being was ever more anxiously waited on than this most popular of Turf favourites.

Now that slumming in the East End is no longer fashionable among ladies of Society, the new idea is to bring the East End to the West, so that problems of poverty may be studied in Mayfair without the attendant inconvenience of going to Stepney. Mrs Carl Meyer [the late Adele Lady Meyer], wife of the financier, has sent me an invitation to a course of lectures and poverty demonstrations at her house in Stratton Street. Mrs Meyer, who is a most thorough social reformer, secured women like Mrs Edwin Gray, president of the National Union of Women Workers, Miss Ravenhill, hygiene lecturer of King's College, Miss MacArthur, Women's Trade Union League, and Miss Hinton Smith, to lecture to the marchionesses and countesses on social problems. Most useful.

The unexpected death of Mr Alfred Baldwin, MP, chairman of the Great Western Railway, creates a vacancy in the Bewdley Division of Worcestershire, and the Central Office tell me it will probably be filled without a contest by Mr. Baldwin's son, Stanley, whom I met the other day with his cousin, Rudyard Kipling. The late MP was a brother-in-law of Sir Edward Burne-Jones, the painter, of Sir Edward Poynter, president of the Royal Academy, and Mr Lockwood Kipling, the artist father of Rudyard Kipling.

The Germans are 'mapping out' East Anglia for future reference. I learned tonight that several mysterious strangers – one of whom I have met near my own place in north-west Essex – have been bicycling and driving and photographing all over the county, particularly along the coast, making sketches and taking notes. Looks like a staff ride. The War Office has been told about these activities. Every time a report is made the spying ceases mysteriously, and then a week or two later it begins again. There is little doubt that the German Army is well represented in East Anglia; but every time I call attention to their spy system I am assailed by the Radicals and called a mischief-maker.

There was a fairly substantial case of spying several years ago. A German who spent most of his time bicycling about, lost a note-book, and it was eventually handed over to the police. The book contained full details of haystacks and barns between Dunmow and Clacton. It was sent to the military authorities, and the undoubted spy was merely warned to be more careful!

February 16, 1908.

I met Mr Cody, the aeronaut, at Charing Cross on my way down. He is engaged, with Colonel Capper in building a new airship for the Army. Says it will be larger than the damaged Nulli Secundus, and that it will attain a speed of forty miles an hour. We chatted about his beginnings as an aeronaut. He came to England ten years ago as a Wild West showman; made himself up to look like 'Buffalo Bill' Cody; to the accompaniment of long hair, sombrero, lariats, revolvers, mustangs, red Indians, and all. Then he took to kite flying for amusement, and became an expert; so that in due course the British Government picked him up and set him up as such at Farnborough, with a salary of £1,000 a year. He has cut off his flowing locks, and now he looks merely like an expert and not a cowboy.

I saw Queen Alexandra in the afternoon driving down the Mall in an open carriage, no doubt owing to the extraordinarily warm weather. She is one of the most remarkably well preserved women I have ever seen. There was the usual crowd of admiring women at the gates of the Palace.

There was a meeting in my room at the *Daily Express* offices this morning for the purpose of co-co-ordinating the opposition to Socialist teaching. The idea is to form a society to be called the Anti-Socialist Union. Its object is to collect facts and figures and train public speakers to counteract the fallacious statements so persistently put about by Socialist writers and speakers, particularly those who speak in parks and open spaces. There is no organisation at present to take up this important work. Those present at the meeting were Mr Claude Lowther, Mr Harry Cust, Lord Abinger, Mr Wilfrid Ashley, MP, Captain Jessel [Lord Jessel], Mr W. H. Mallock, and myself. Mr Mallock, who is the foremost authority on the subject, is to be the first secretary of the Union, and Mr F. E. Smith, KC, MP [Earl of Birkenhead], is to address the first public meeting at the Caxton Hall.

Mr A. J. Wilson, who knows all about cycling, says there is going to be a boom in tricycles this year. The Humbers, for instance, are making a tricycle which is only a little heavier than an ordinary bicycle, and it is expected that elderly people who do not like either motorcars or bicycles, will take to the new tricycle as a means of obtaining exercise. The roads are full enough already of all sorts of new-fangled traffic without this added infliction.

February 17, 1908.

Sam Evans, now metamorphosed into Sir Samuel, took over his post of Solicitor-General today, much to the envy of other Liberal lawyers in the House, for the Solicitor earns something like £ 15,000 a year. I wrote him a note of congratulation to the House of Commons, and he answered characteristically: 'I would rather have your job than mine, because my employers are more exacting. Besides, I may lose it at any moment through no fault of my own.

Edwin Cleary, the never-faltering impressario, traveller, actor, contractor, correspondent, and general favourite, was entertaining a party of friends with some of his astonishing experiences today. He is off to America tomorrow in search of adventure, with half a dozen new patents in his bag. He proposes to go by way of Glasgow to New York, since the fare first class is only £12 10s, whereas one cannot go from London, Liverpool, or Southampton for much less than £20 first-class.

At Romano's at lunch I met Jimmy Welch, the actor, who has been ill and out of the cast of *When Knights Were Bold*, at Wyndham's. Welch was contemptuous about kinematograph shows, which appear to be frightening other theatrical folk. He does not think they can ever compete with the legitimate stage, and that in any case the music hall has nothing to fear from moving pictures as a means of a full-programme entertainment. The music hall, he says, will absorb the moving picture, and in the meantime the variety stage will be improved by the absorption of legitimate actors. In confirmation, he pointed to the fact that Constance Collier, so well known in connection with Beerbohm Tree's productions, is to go to the Empire next week, and that Ruth Vincent is leaving the regular stage for a turn at the Palace.

Coming home along the Embankment at midnight, with Arthur Pearson, from Blackfriars as far as Northumberland

Avenue, we counted fifteen homeless couples, evidently married out-of-works. Three of them had children with them, and of these two were barefooted; which was unusual even in this haunt of the unfortunate. The Salvation Army people were handing out hot soup to the miserable folk. This midnight poverty of London is one of the most pathetic sights of the metropolis.

More new fashions. Shearn, the florist, informs me that imitation blossoms made of feathers are now worn for hat trimmings. Rosettes of Parma violets, of imitation ostrich feathers, are favourite. He showed me a large black 'crinoline' picture hat, made to order. Round the crown swept a fine long feather made of imitation flowers.

Pruger, the manager of the Savoy, says that it is only in the past ten years that English men and women have thought of going to hotel restaurants to dine. When he first came to London only foreigners went to the hotels for entertainment and food. The 'natives' either entertained their friends at home or at clubs. As for ladies, there were only half a dozen places, such as the Café Royal, Scott's, Verrey's, the Amphitron, Prince's Willis', or Simpson's in the Strand.

1909

Wednesday, January 27, 1909.

I went to the first night of *An Englishman's Home* tonight. A great patriotic play which is certain to rouse controversy. The author's name is not given, but I know him to be Captain Guy du Maurier, son of the author of *Trilby* and brother of Gerald du Maurier, the actor. He is an officer on the active list in the Royal Fusiliers, and, of course, he cannot permit his name to appear. The plot of the play is along the lines of Lord Roberts' preaching against unpreparedness.

In the lobby of the theatre I met Lord Charles Beresford, who tells me that he will have to retire from the command of the Channel Fleet next month. He was not very complimentary about his rival, Admiral Fisher, who, he says, is doing everything in his power to wreck the British Navy. 'Mark my word', said Lord Charles, 'if we ever go to war with Germany, and Fisher remains as First Sea Lord and has anything to do with the disposition of the Fleet, we will suffer disaster.'

AUGUST

Tuesday, August 25, 1909.

Had a visit this evening from Lieutenant Ernest Shackleton, the explorer, who has just returned from the Antarctic. He is anxious that the Government or some private person should give him money enough to go on another expedition, and thinks that £20,000 would be sufficient. Shackleton thinks there is much more to be got out of an expedition of this sort than can be had from financing, say, these spectacular attempts at flying the Channel by flying machine. Only today, for instance, Monsieur Paulhan flew eighty-two miles continuously, which shows that the flying machine is no longer a toy in the hands of an expert; but what is the use of expending large sums of these trans-Channel flights that always come to grief, except in proper hands?

Thus, last week M. Bleriot flew the Channel in half an hour – thirty-three minutes to be exact. Mr H. Latham has tried it twice and failed. The first time he fell into the sea and was rescued by following vessels. I agree with Shackleton that these things represent a foolish waste of money. Besides, flying across the Channel means nothing after you have done it. You can't carry goods or passengers.

Monday, August 29, 1909.

Sir George Arthur came in and showed me a letter which he had just received from Lord Kitchener. He writes that he has been going about with Maxwell [Sir John] and Birdwood [the Soul of Anzac] to look for a house. 'I must have somewhere to lay my head.' As to employment, he adds, 'I am only a "Has Been", and I am afraid there is nothing for me in England. – Yours ever, K.' I wrote a line to Sir Arthur Bigge [Lord Stamfordham], and started an agitation for K.'s employment.

Then went to the Admiralty to see Sir W. Grahame Greene, the Permanent Secretary, and asked him to issue some sort of official statement about the two British officers, Brandon and Trench, whom the Germans have locked up as British spies. One of them is R. N. and the other a Marine. We refrained from printing their names last night, but it would be wise for the Admiralty to tell the public that these men are not spies. Greene professes never to have heard of them, and referred me to the Foreign Office. I said it was no business of mine to clear up their muddles for them, and went away. But I went to the F. O. They were very polite, but very nervous. No one wants to know anything about the officers!

I dined this evening at the Travellers' with Major-General the Hon. Julian Byng, who is my usual Sunday morning walking companion over the ploughed fields of Essex, when we discuss Conscription, Clausewitz, Stonewall Jackson, Boy Scouts, and Woman's Suffrage. He commands the East Anglian Territorial Division, one of the youngest and wisest generals in the Army. He ought to go a long way.

I have lately been receiving some intensely abusive letters from a rabid Socialist named Ervine, who writes me long missives which, if true, make me out to be one of the worst men alive. His English is, anyhow, most vigorous and vivid and picturesque, and I finally wrote and asked him to come and call on me. I wanted to see what sort of crabbed, bitter, disappointed old man I had to deal with. At first he demurred; said that, 'true to type', I would have him assaulted by my hired ruffians. But at last he agreed. He came this afternoon. Instead of a wild-eyed bomb-thrower, there came into my room a charming Irish youth with curly reddish hair, a winning smile and a shy manner. His name is St John Ervine; he comes from Ulster, and he has literary aspirations. He was practising on me.

Coronation Day on Thursday of this week and Honours List sent out to newspapers this evening. This always gives me opportunity of being first to send messages of congratulation to any friends who happen to be in the list. They do not understand how it is that they receive my telegram simultaneously with the announcement in the morning papers. ignorant of the fact that I have twelve hours' start of the public. So tonight I had occasion to send a message to young Max Aitken, who came over here from Canada last autumn, won a sensational parliamentary victory at Ashton-under-Lyne within a few months of his arrival, and now becomes a knight, all in record time. He shows a natural aptitude for politics and newspapers, and insists that he and I are going to do big things together.

I remember meeting him for the first time last September, at a luncheon given by Edward Goulding and several others to Arthur Balfour and Bonar Law. He told me then that he proposed winning a difficult seat, and I did not believe he would do it.

1911

Monday, June 10, 1911.

This was Coronation Day. I reached the Abbey at seven o'clock this morning and found my place high up in the Triforium, from which there was a splendid view, I sat entranced throughout the morning until two o'clock. It was the most wonderful sight of my life. Pageant after pageant, picture after picture unrolling before our eyes. I do not think it is possible to put one's emotions into words. The vast area covered with gorgeous costumes, colours, flowers, blazoned on all sides, procession on procession all culminating in the wonderful coronation scenes. I think the thing which impressed me most was when the young Prince of Wales appeared before his royal father to do obeisance as those before him had done. The young prince stepped forward and bowed low before his father. Sweeping his robes of the Garter to each side as he advanced up the steps of the throne, he knelt down and said, 'I, Edward Prince of Wales, do become your liege man of life and limb and of earthly worship; and faith and truth I will bear unto you, to live and die against all manner of folks. So help me God.'

The boy touched the royal crown with his forefinger and then kissed the King on the left cheek. Custom prescribes this. But as he got up the parent reached out his hand and drew his son to him and kissed him; and the boy, overcome for the moment, kissed the King's hand and hurried away. Just a simple English boy.

In the evening I went to the Native Exhibition at the White City, but there was such a crowd it was almost impossible to move, so I came away.

1912

Friday, March 29, 1912.

A letter from Rudyard Kipling about the future, in which he says,'This summer, if I live, sees me clear of coal, and five years will see one third of England equally clear. In ten years the miners will work "with but after" jewellers and engravers.' From which I take it that the Electric Age will be all prevailing in 1922.

Winston Churchill rang me up to explain his policy of holding up the Budget by £6,500,000, as he knows that Germany proposes to expand her fleet, and that we must be ready to meet that expansion. It is curious how all these people are harping on the same subject.

Came up in the same train as the Countess of Warwick, who was travelling third class! The world is indeed changing.

MAY

Tuesday, May 7, 1912.

Lunching today with three or four people, including Sir Edward Carson [Lord Carson], and, talking about Asquith's proposal to make 100 Liberal peers if Home Rule Bill is defeated. Carson said he had been dining with an August Personage, who said: 'I think, Sir Edward, it is too bad that certain members of the House of Commons should show so much animosity towards individuals. There, for instance, some one said rude things to the great and good man, Mr——'

'Well,' said Carson in reply, 'your great and good Mr —— is a downright scamp and a vicious and dirty liar.' Carson also said how he had encountered the Lord Chief Justice, Lord Alverstone, who said to him in connection with the Die-Hard business, 'Carson, I'm ashamed of you.'

'Well, chief', Oi said to him, 'it's manny a toime Oi've been ashamed of you, too!' Carson tells me he is sacrificing £20,000 a year at the Bar to look after the Ulster campaign.

JULY

Tuesday, July 9, 1912.

Wonderful Naval Review at Spithead today. Over 300 ships in the fleet. I went in the Admiralty yacht *Enchantress* as guest of Winston Churchill, First Lord of the Admiralty. Many people of note on board, including the Prime Minister and Mrs Asquith, Admirals Beatty and Troubridge, General Sir John French, and Sir Ernest Cassel. When the fleet passed out, Winston, on the bridge, took the salute, which some of the naval folk on board said he should not have done.

Came home in the evening in a special train with General Sir John French, who was quite garrulous, and soon got on his pet aversion, Kitchener. French suffers from some slight, imaginary or otherwise, suffered at Lord K.'s hands in the Boer War. He told me how once, when public opinion in South Africa seemed to be against him, Lord K. had come to him and went and 'carried on' like a young schoolgirl, great big chap that he was. French said further, 'Lord Roberts is a kindly gentleman, but he did no good in South Africa. I had the Boers in the hollow of my hand on two occasions, and each time "Bobs" stopped me and let them slip away. I could have ended the war long before.'

French ambled on like this all the way to London, and if a stranger had heard him, not knowing him to be a gallant, chivalrous and brilliant leader, he would have been put down as a village gossip.

Saturday, July 27, 1912.

A great Unionist demonstration at Blenheim, the Duke of Marlborough's seat in Oxfordshire. About 15,000 people gathered in the open before the great palace to hear Bonar Law, the new leader, and F. E. Smith. I am remaining in the house party, which includes the Duke and Duchess of Norfolk, Viscount Churchill, Lord Balcarres, Harry Lawson [Viscount Burnham], Mr and Mrs F. E. Smith, Edward Goulding [Lord Wargrave], Bonar Law, Carson, James Campbell [Lord Glenavy], Lady Sarah Wilson, Lord and Lady Midleton. Sitting in the hall after the speeches Bonar said to 'F. E.,' with a twinkle in his eye, 'I've got some bad news for you "F. E.", I'm getting to be quite fond of leadership.' F. E. smilingly retorted, 'That's all right. I can afford to wait.'

SEPTEMBER

Monday, September 16, 1912.

When I came down from Cumberland recently on the Great North Road I appeared to encounter an enormous number of cheap foreign cars, so I determined to see if we could not establish the popularity of British made cars over the machines produced by foreign countries. I gave a luncheon at the Ritz Hotel to representatives of seventeen British automobile manufacturing companies, with Lord Montague in the chair. Among others present were Mr S. F. Edge, Mr Charles Jarrott, Mr W. M. Letts, Sir Charles Friswell, Mr J. Thorneycroft, Mr Sidney Straker, Mr F. Lanchester, Mr Holt Thomas, and Mr Thornton Rutter. There were many speeches, and the result of this gathering was the determination to form a £5 million company – in the United States this would be called a 'trust' – to fight the foreign automobile invasion. It is proposed to manufacture a machine that will be nearly as cheap and quite as good as – some said better than – the American product.

A letter was read from the Duke of Westminster, in which he said that the invasion of the American cars 'threaten to deprive thousands of English workers of employment, and the way out is to start a vigorous campaign throughout the country to advance the cause of British Imperial preference.

1913

Tuesday, February 25, 1913.

Someone, somewhere, has started a story about mysterious airships which fly over the country at night. No one has yet seen them, but people at various points along the East and South coasts profess to have heard them. The Army authorities put no credence in them, but in a chat I had today with Colonel Marker, Coldstream Guards, he said it would not be surprising if the Germans were making secret night passages with the secret airships. They have been carrying out staff rides on the East coast for years without hindrance. Why not air rides? On the other hand, one could see as well as hear them, and no one has yet seen them.

APRIL

Sunday, April 13, 1913.

Supper at H. G. Wells's in Easton Park. H. G. gave a most interesting dissertation on politics. His belief is that the Liberal Party is more dead than the Tory Party, and that both are dead beyond recall.

Thursday, April 24, 1913.

Lunching today at the club, Sir J. Henniker Heaton, the postal reformer, said, 'Within three years there will leave daily from the G. P. O. airships for Bombay, Cairo, Paris, Berlin and so on.' He prefers penny postage to a Channel tunnel; more useful.

SEPTEMBER

Wednesday, September 3, 1913.

The Kabaka (King of Buganda), a pleasant white-robed young black potentate from Africa, came to the *Daily Express* offices at eleven o'clock this evening with four of his chiefs and a British officer in attendance. I showed them round, and was as much interested in their exhibitions of surprise as they were at what they saw. One of the chiefs described the office as 'a storehouse of knowledge'. I think he must have been primed to say that, for whenever he came within whispering distance of me he said, 'Storehouse of Knowledge.' Otherwise he spoke no English. The Kabaka is seventeen years old and a Christian.

At lunch today with Bertrand Stewart, a yeomanry officer who had just been released by the Germans after two years of really brutal imprisonment on the charge of espionage. They had him in solitary confinement for weeks, and his imprisonment was due wholly to political reasons. The Government here were supine. Never made the slightest attempt to have him released for fear of offending the dear All Highest. [Captain Stewart, on General Allenby's staff, was killed shortly after the outbreak of the Great War.]

1914

The year 1914 began with evil portents. The situation in Ireland had reached its climax, and the fear of civil war dominated all conversation. Sir Edward Carson stood out as the most formidable person in the Empire. One half of the people looked upon him as a sinister figure; the other worshipped him. In the North of Ireland crowds followed him muttering prayers for his preservation; women kissed his hand and held children up for him to touch them against illness. The Great War to break out this year was only spoken of as a possibility of the dim future and then only by the so-called 'Scaremongers', who sought preparedness, the Diarist, among them. Society was having a good time. Here is an extract:

Saturday, March 1914.

Sir Edward Carson came down to Dunmow to stay with me for the weekend. We stopped for a few minutes in the High Street. Instantly the car was surrounded. 'God bless you, sir', 'God give you strength', and so on from all sides. Carson says that Asquith would like to get out of his difficulties if he could, but circumstances are against him.

They have got the names of twenty-eight leaders to be arrested at a favourable moment. That would mean instant war. 'The fact is', he says, 'I am so much concerned about the pressure which is being put on us by the Government that I am seriously thinking of calling out our Ulster Army.'

Friday, March 20, 1914.

Carson walked out of the House of Commons yesterday 'to go to my people' in Ulster. Meanwhile there are rumours that troops have been ordered to Ulster from the South of Ireland, and that a number of officers have resigned since they refuse to take part in a civil war. Late tonight we learn that the entire Third Cavalry Brigade at the Curragh, commanded by Major-General Hubert Gough, has refused to move. The officers were given their choice of going or being dismissed, and they chose the latter. This dishes Winston.

Sunday, March 22, 1914.

Came up to town. Things most exciting. General Henry Wilson, Director of Military Operations, told me the entire Army Council were threatening to resign if pressure was not taken off Gough and he and his officers restored. I went to the War Office. The place was seething with excitement. Saw General French, who resigns and does not resign. He does not know what to do. 'Jack' Seeley, the War Minister, will become the scapegoat. Opposition leaders, Bonar Law, Lansdowne, Devonshire, Salisbury, have been in consultation all the morning at Lansdowne House.

Monday, March 23, 1914.

Asquith tells *The Times* that it was not meant seriously and so on. Arthur Paget, C.-in-C. Ireland, is now becoming the Government's scapegoat, but his brother Almeric [Lord Queenborough] tells me the general will hit back if they try to implicate him. Meanwhile Seely announces in the House that Gough and his officers have been ordered to resume. 'Misunderstandings, etc.' – I met Colonel John Gough, Hubert's twin brother, who informed me that they had got a written undertaking from Jack Seely and General Ewart that troops would not be used against Ulster. Lloyd George is furious. General French and General Ewart keep on resigning, though all the Cabinet Ministers deny it in turn. All topsy-turvy. But tonight Seely has actually gone and French has definitely resigned again. Carson over in Ireland drilling his troops with wooden guns.

APRIL–JUNE

By April the Ulster Army was an effective force and was regularly receiving arms through the process of gun running.

Saturday, April 11, 1914.

Arrived in Belfast this morning and watched a regiment of volunteers under Colonel E. L. E. Malone, a regular officer, drill in the grounds of Belfast Castle. They were splendid material. Went on to Lady Masserene's house party at Antrim Castle. Large party assembled for lunch from Mount Stewart, Lord and Lady Midleton, Mr Wilfrid Ashley, MP, Mr Edmund Gosse, the Bishop of Down, Colonel Hacket Pain, Colonel Sharman-Crawford, the Duchess of Montrose, Sir R. Hermon-Hodge [Lord Wyfold], Captain Craig [Lord Craigavon], Ronald McNeill [Lord Cushendun], Mr and Mrs H. A. Gwynne. All assembled to witness a presentation of colours to the South Antrim regiment, of which Arthur Pakenham is colonel and Wilfrid Ashley adjutant.

Tuesday, April 14, 1914.

At Clandeboye, Lord Dufferin's place, to attend a review of half a dozen Ulster regiments. Very fine military display. It now seems certain that these people mean to fight.

On Saturday, April 25, the country was startled by the report of a wholesale gun running exploit which took place in Ulster. The whole volunteer force took part. They 'ran in 30,000 rifles and over 3 million rounds. Police and military helpless. That finally established the Ulster force as a strong card in future negotiations, for it was rifles and guns that were lacking up to now. We can now hope for decent peace terms,' says the Diary, 'and so avoid the dread civil war which has been hanging over the two countries.'

The outcome was a Home Rule conference between both sides. It took place at Buckingham Palace, and went on for weeks. In June the bomb that killed the Austrian heir to the throne and his wife at Sarajevo was the first act of the Great War. We in England knew it not, and cared not. Ulster was more important.

Sunday, June 28, 1914.

H. G. Wells came over to tea. While we were talking, news came that Austria's Crown Prince and his wife have been assassinated by a Serbian. That will mean war. Wells says it will mean more than that. It will set the world alight. I don't see why the world should fight over the act of a lunatic.

JULY

Ulster still uppermost. Many lunches and dinners. Covenanters' Clubs, Women's Committees, Collections, and fervent oratory. General gaiety as well, and women beginning to go to prize fights such as that between Bombardier Wells and Colin Bell and Carpentier and 'Gunboat' Smith.

Thursday July 16, 1914.

Sat with Lord Rosebery, his son, Neil Primrose and
Max Aitken. Lord Rosebery not much impressed with
the unskilfulness of 'Gunboat,' who was disqualified for
striking Carpentier while he was half-way on the floor.

Friday, July 24, 1914.

Ulster situation terribly gloomy. Conference likely to be
ineffective, and we are getting closer to civil war. Dinner
tonight at Mrs Rupert Beckett's, where all present seemed
to reflect the situation in their talk. Continental affairs
not discussed, although Austria will probably declare
war on Serbia to-morrow. At dinner there were Bonar
Law, Carson with Miss Frewen, whom he is to marry,
F. E. Smith and Lady Smith, Lord and Lady Londonderry,
Ronald McNeill, Mr and Mrs Rochfort Maguire,
Mrs Ralph Sneyd, and the Duchess of Westminster. Civil
war inevitable, they all say. 'A fortnight from now', says
Maguire, 'and we'll all be in the middle of it unless a
miracle intervenes.'

Sunday, July 26, 1914.

Collision in Dublin between Scottish Borderers and a mob
over gun-running. Four killed, seventy wounded. This puts
the lid on!

*On the Continent things were seething. On Tuesday, July 28,
panics everywhere. Austria, France, Germany, and Russia
getting ready. Belgrade evacuated. In England the Home Rule
Amending Bill was put down for passage on the following
Thursday. Newspaper circulations were rising, but advertising
going to bits.*

Wednesday, July 29, 1914.

Mr Selfridge came down to see me at night to hear the latest news. He did not think the Germans would care to go to war. 'They can't stand it financially', he said, 'they wouldn't last till Christmas.' I retorted that, nevertheless, we were beginning to take notice, and had got so far that we are not printing the movements of the Army and Navy units.

Thursday, July 30, 1914.

Belgrade on fire. Tension. Many failures. Asquith announces a truce on Home Rule owing to the situation. 'Britain's united front and so on.' Liberal clamour to keep clear. We are urging the Government not to let France down.

Friday, July 31, 1914.

T. P. O'Connor asked me in the morning to see Carson and get him to offer 'a golden bridge' on which he and Redmond could meet. I went to Carson in Eaton Place at 11.30am He was in bed with a headache. 'The only golden bridge I'll offer', he said, 'is give me a clean cut of Ulster.'

Drew my salary in gold for this month and then changed it again to paper. Will not do to hoard gold now.

AUGUST

Saturday, August 1, 1914.

Went down home to Easton with our *Daily Express* cricket eleven to play Easton Lodge. We were beaten. After match we learned that Germany had declared war on Russia and had marched into Luxemburg, thus violating her treaty engagements. If this country does not stand up for Right and Honour she will be forever damned.

Sunday, August 2, 1914.

Had a visit this morning from Herr Kurt Buetow, the German tutor to Mr H. G. Wells's two boys. [This is the famous German tutor in *Mr Britling Sees It Through*] He came to bid us goodbye, since he has been called home to Germany to take his place in the Army. He was very stiff and formal and polite, but evidently sorry to leave England.

Came up to town early. In St James's Park, just below the German Embassy, I met Prince Lichnowski, the German Ambassador, looking terribly sad. 'I am afraid we can do no more', he said. 'I have just seen Sir Edward Grey, and you are likely to take sides with the French.' Moratorium to be declared tomorrow. No debt settlements. So there'll be no money panics.

Monday, August 3, 1914.

Sir E. Grey leaves no doubt as to British course. Declares in Commons that he will fight if the French coast is harried. Mobilisation decided on. Crowds in streets, and the Germans are on the Belgian Frontier.

Tuesday, August 4, 1914.

Ultimatum sent to Germany to respect Belgian neutrality. It expires at midnight. Declined, so there is nothing for it. At midnight Great Britain declared war on Germany.

We are in it! How long?